Fresh Approaches to Working With Problematic Behavior

By Adele M. Brodkin, Ph.D.

Edited by Jane Schall

SCHOLASTIC
PROFESSIONAL BOOKS

NEW YORK • TORONTO • LONDON • AUCKLAND • SYDNEY
MEXICO CITY • NEW DELHI • HONG KONG • BUENOS AIRES

For Helen H. Meyer,

my mother and first teacher,

with admiration and the deepest affection.

ACKNOWLEDGMENTS

I want, first of all, to express my thanks to Dick Robinson and Helen Benham for opening Scholastic's door and making me feel welcome. Every minute of my long association with the Scholastic family has been deeply gratifying. As the teachers who helped to make this book a reality know, there is no greater gift than the opportunity to make even the smallest contribution to one's world.

Terry Cooper deserves more thank-yous than I can give her for her faith and dogged insistence that I could write this book. Thanks are due to Wendy Murray for her patience, steadfastness, and for seeing to it that I faced the practical realities of this task. A great big thank-you goes to the editor, Jane Schall, for being a generous friend, for sharing her rare vision and remarkable skills, and for her readiness to reassure me, no matter what.

Last, but by far, not the least, I thank the teachers who gave their time, shared their successes and non-successes, as well as their insights, and who trusted us with their feelings. Out of respect for confidentiality, we cannot name those teachers or use the actual names of children, but we will always remember them and be grateful for who they are.

No part of this publication may be reproduced in whole or in part, or stored in a retrieval system, or transmitted in any form or by any means, electronic, mechanical, photocopying, recording, or otherwise, without permission of the publisher. For information regarding permission, write to Scholastic Permissions, 555 Broadway, New York, NY 10012-3999.

Front cover and interior design by Kathy Massaro
Cover photos: Top photo courtesy of Dynamic Graphics. Others by Vicky Kasala.

ISBN 0-590-03005-1
Copyright © 2001 by Adele M. Brodkin
All rights reserved.
Printed in the U.S.A.

CONTENTS

IT WAS SOME TIME AGO that Terry Cooper, vice president and editor-in-chief at Scholastic, first approached me about writing a book for teachers who are faced with the bewildering challenge of problematic behavior in their classrooms. Both of us were acutely aware that a growing number of children are so preoccupied with personal issues that it is difficult for them to concentrate on learning, but when Terry turned to me for answers I felt rather unequal to the task. Yes, I am a student of and a teacher of child development. I spent many years practicing school psychology and consulting with hospital pediatric departments, prevention programs such as Head Start, parents, and teachers in urban, suburban, and rural communities. Throughout my career, however, my own work has been with one child at a time. For years I have admired teachers' remarkable capacity to have "eyes and ears on all sides of their heads." How could I possibly tell them how to use their classrooms as agents of behavioral change?

In time Terry and I were joined by Scholastic Professional Books editor Wendy Murray, all three of us then reflecting about how I might advise teachers. Happily, one fortunate day, Terry said she thought they might have come upon an answer: Seek the advice of teachers who have wrestled with these dilemmas and won, at least some of the time. With Terry's and Wendy's guidance, I got to work. We reached out to teachers early on through Scholastic's Internet site, then through a small sample of the vast network of Scholastic's teacher-advisors and consultants in the United States and Canada. We began by asking for detailed examples of problematic behavior, and as we listened, two broad categories emerged: The first, "disruptive behavior," includes calling out, clowning, making silly noises, getting up and doing intrusive or distracting things (thereby interfering with others' ability to work), rowdiness in the halls and/or playground, bossiness, disrespectfulness, overall poor self-control, verbal or physical aggression, and various other thinly disguised pleas for attention. The second category we call "disappearing behavior." While it is not as intrusive, it is at least as worrisome as disruptiveness and includes a child's tuning out, being lost "in a private world," daydreaming, not listening, avoiding participation (due to extreme timidity), and having little or no apparent pride in one's work or interest in social surroundings.

Listening to and discussing these teachers' stories spurred me on. The issues were vital, not only for current classroom situations, but also for so many children's futures. I thought about research, which indicates that "disruptiveness" is often associated with social rejection. I also considered the fact that both disruptiveness and social isolation not only interfere with learning, but are positively associated with future problems, ranging from dropping out of school to enduring serious adjustment difficulties in adulthood. Therefore, I knew how high the stakes were for these children, and I was eager to pursue the matter further. What began as a few exploratory telephone conversations broadened into a series of captivating interviews. And what began as a scientific report became a compilation of some amazing teachers' wisdom, experiences, and insights.

But I am getting ahead of myself, for before this project could become anything like what I've described, it needed the vital collaboration of Jane Schall. Terry, Wendy, Jane, and I studied the remarkable transcripts of the interviews. We talked, and thought, and reviewed the teachers' words. Then Jane devised the organization we would need to create our book. This was a Herculean task.

I offer you here a brief overview of what we learned, that is, a preview of what awaits you in the pages ahead. The teachers described children who entered their classrooms with many needs unmet, which resulted in a variety of problematic behaviors. Common themes began to emerge—themes that revealed similar insights about what was behind differing problematic behaviors and about what worked to effect change. For example, those who succeeded much of the time reported the benefits of acknowledging the positive qualities of the children in question. According to the teachers, progress began when they repeatedly expressed genuine belief in these children's capacity to change and to succeed. Taking the time to observe and get to know each child as an individual was considered an essential first step.

There were common themes, but every child's situation called for a uniquely designed intervention. The teachers tuned in and found what some called the "hook" to welcome each child into the fold of the classroom. This meant discovering each child's special interests and wishes. Through these "hooks" the teachers found ways for kids to be and feel successful. In many cases the children gradually became more comfortable with themselves as integral members of the group.

These teachers trusted their own instincts, their own zeal, and took chances on children with problematic histories. They collaborated with the children and, if at all possible, with the families. Without being intrusive, they did everything they could to get to know the child's situation outside of school. Whenever possible, they worked very hard to find the "hook" for parents, too, in an effort to make parents feel comfortable and supported.

The teachers told us about the value of starting the year off with a mutual trust and understanding between teacher and child, a warm classroom ambience, and a consistent presentation of expectations. While some studied past records and eagerly sought out the counsel of former teachers, others purposely avoided the risk of prejudging a child. All came to their own conclusions about the problems and how to address them. To a person, every teacher discovered the power of positive reward and recognition as well as the importance of cultivating a capacity for empathy in themselves and their students. They saw some of the parents benefit from teacher support, but above all, they and the children reaped the rewards of making the classroom an oasis of calm, caring, and positive expectations, no matter what a child faced in the outside world.

These teachers were bravely honest with themselves. They grappled with concerns about "burning out," but even more with the painful recognition that "you can't win them all." The teachers knew that sometimes they had to come to terms with the fact that they could not turn a particular child's life around. I suspect, however, that they may have had a far greater impact than they will ever know.

Fortunately, all of the teachers acknowledged their own needs for support and counsel, especially from their peers. They did not hesitate to call upon their districts' resources, reaching out to special-service team members with whom they had positive relationships, or calling on administrators, and especially on close friends who were also colleagues. Many set an example by suggesting how valuable it is to get to know and draw on the expertise of support staff and child-study team members who are available in their districts. Of course, in a perfect world, a child in need is evaluated by a gifted and motivated team of experts including a psycho-diagnostician, a child psychiatrist, a developmental pediatrician, possibly a pediatric neurologist, an occupational therapist, as well as a learning specialist. Then in concert with the teacher and parents, a plan is drawn up—perhaps private counseling, perhaps tutoring, or any other appropriate interventions in areas such as speech or occupational therapy. The teacher and parents also have their role to play in the remediation plan.

But it is not a perfect world, and in some settings, nothing is available that might approach the above ideal, so teachers too often have only themselves to draw on. As long as they know that is not the way it ought to be and are aware of their professional limitations (they are trained as educators), they can be cautious and seek whatever guidance is available in their particular districts and schools.

As you join these forthright teachers in the pages ahead, think of them as your close friends, who are also colleagues. You will find that no one school of thought or philosophy emerged as their key to success. They have no concrete cookbook of "How-tos" or "What to do whens." What they do have is wisdom, based on reflection and a sincere search for the truth.

One final note: This book does not focus on children with measurable learning disabilities, certified special needs, or children with organic syndromes or DSMIV diagnoses, although some of the children discussed happen to have been so identified. Instead, it is simply about children whose classroom behavior has been problematic for themselves and/or others. It is about their teachers finding ways of bringing them into the comfortable mainstream of classroom life.

Getting to Know Children

I N T H I S C H A P T E R we consider two forms of problematic behavior. The first is seen in children who are disruptive, and the second among children who turn inward and avoid social contact. Of course, there is much more to know about any given child with problematic behavior. As these teachers' stories clearly demonstrate, each child must be listened to and understood as an individual. These teachers' inclination to listen and tune in to individual children has been essential to their success.

Children Who Are Disruptive

When we think of problematic behavior, disruptive children are generally the first to come to mind. Let's begin with an example provided by a primary level teacher:

MAKING EXPECTATIONS CLEAR

Stuart was a first grader who just didn't understand the rules of the classroom. I think it was because he didn't have a predictable or reliable home life and therefore didn't understand structure. He had already been in three different kindergarten classes and had come to us after about the

> "Each of my students is precious, and each gets one slice of what we have in the classroom. A child who is brilliant, a child who is extremely disruptive—neither gets a disproportionate amount. Everyone has a right to the most. Everybody has a right to thrive."
>
> —fourth-grade teacher

fourth week of school, so he had missed the big stuff I do to explain classroom expectations. It wasn't long before the other kids resented him because he just had no clue of how to behave.

I soon realized that I would have to spell out what was expected of him in each setting, each hour of the day. When his behavior was inappropriate, we would talk: "Is this a good time for you to call out?" "Is this a good time for you to get up and walk around?" It took a lot of effort on my part, but eventually he came to understand the behavior that was expected of him— when and where.

DR. BRODKIN COMMENTS

Happily, the approach this teacher chose was effective with this particular child and probably would be with a number of others—but not for every expressive or impulsive child. In fact, there are some children who would hear the question, "Is this a good time for you to call out?" and think of it as a challenge, an invitation to be even more provocative. Such children might respond, "Yes, it is!" and behave accordingly. This brings us to one of the most important lessons of this book: Different approaches work for different children. What's more, each teacher-child pair is unique. It pays to experiment and to be flexible. When you do, you're more likely to find an approach that works, as was the case for this teacher in the next part of her story. A determined search led to her discovering the key to motivating this student.

At our school we have classroom points, or "dollars," children can earn so they can buy things at our store—pencils, pens, etc.—once a week. Stuart liked having the dollars, so I decided to use that fact to motivate him to concentrate on specific behaviors. For instance, one day we would focus on calling or speaking out. I'd tell him that if he didn't call out for three hours, he would earn one dollar for each of the hours. After each hour we'd take a break, a sort of recess, and I would try to encourage him by saying, "Remember, if you can make it without calling out for another hour you'll earn another dollar." Before long I realized that Stuart seemed to need the money in his hand to be motivated, so I decided to give him all three dollars at once and say, "Each time you call out, I will take a dollar away." Lo and behold: That worked. He could see the money, and he knew that if he spoke out, I was going to get one of those dollars back.

We worked on only one behavioral issue at a time. We tackled getting up and walking around, and then we moved on to bodily contact, which was another big problem for him. He couldn't keep his hands or his body to himself.

I also made helping Stuart catch on to our preferred way of behaving a classroom project. "We've got to work really hard to help Stuart," I'd tell the class, "because he wants to do his best, but he doesn't always remember the rules. We have to help him." I told his group in particular, "You've got to work hard with Stuart; you've got to give him signals so he remembers what he needs to do." Then, when Stuart did remember, we'd praise him and applaud and say, "Isn't that great!" We'd practically have a party, and that way everyone would rejoice because they had all helped. I could say, "If you hadn't helped, we wouldn't be where we are." In other words, we all shared ownership of helping Stuart become a success, and that left less of the responsibility on me. Stuart helped, too. At the end of the day, no matter what had happened, he'd give me the biggest hug, saying, "I just love you!"

Some days I remember thinking, "You should hate me because I'm at you all day long," but he knew he needed the structure and was grateful for it. It was probably the only structure he had in his life.

We did this for a whole trimester and then we had a long break. When we came back I was concerned that after three weeks on his own, he'd be right back where we started. But the student teacher, who hadn't seen him since the first month of school, said that she saw a wonderful change. When you're living it day-to-day, it's often hard to see progress. It really helps to have someone who has stepped away from the situation give you a clearer picture.

DR. BRODKIN COMMENTS

Flexibility is essential, but paradoxically, we also need to set limits, as this following teacher's story illustrates.

SETTING CLEAR BOUNDARIES

Some children don't understand boundaries, or they don't understand that they're doing something wrong, and these are the individuals, I think, who are hardest to discipline. Whether they have no boundaries at home and therefore don't understand boundaries at school, or whether they actually have some sort of attention difficulty, these children don't seem to know right from wrong. My biggest problem with their disruptive behavior is when it interferes with the learning of other children. One boundary-confused child jumps to my mind, someone I had in class my first year of teaching. This child had many emotional problems and was trying to deal with them. One of the ways he did that was by seeking negative attention. This was a tricky situation to deal with, because while he was deliberately causing a problem, he was also unknowingly crying out for help.

This child, Tony, had already been seen as a "bad guy" before I knew him. But this was my first year teaching, and I wanted to think there was no such thing, so I was looking for alternative explanations. I purposely had a lot of contact with his child-study team; the primary members consisted of a learning consultant, a social worker, and a psychologist. We talked about Tony a lot. I thought he had some solid potential as a learner, but his behavior was getting in the way. He did have some substantial academic issues, but I didn't believe that meant he couldn't do the work. We made a strong commitment to helping Tony, and his parents were wonderful. They helped me understand who he was and supported me, so whether my concern was about his behavior or about his work, school discipline was backed up at home.

* * *

We tried behavior modification, rewarding Tony for calling out "only five times today" as opposed to the seven times that had been typical. And we rewarded him with things he liked to do, such as have a few extra minutes on the computer. We did more positive reinforcement with him than I've ever done with any kid because we found out quickly that he didn't respond to negative reinforcement at all. He would just become more angry. He could get an F on a test and say he didn't care, but of course he did care, and the failure usually made his behavior worse.

It's important to add that this child was incredibly honest. I remember one day when I noticed there were no markers left in the box. I asked the kids where they were. Tony raised his hand and said, "I threw them all out the window." After school Tony and I went out and I sat in a chair and he picked up all the markers that were strewn all over the schoolyard. I think he wanted me to yell at him and fuss. He didn't realize that he wasn't going to get that reaction from me. I also refused to let him think that I was disappointed in him, which was another reaction he expected. It wasn't that I didn't discipline him. It's just that I refused to yell at him and tell him that he had personally disappointed me. Instead I would say, "I'm disappointed that you did *that*." In other words, I expressed disappointment in his behavior, but not in him as a person. And I think he really heard that distinction loud and clear.

I learned that he was a child who had very low expectations of everybody and seemed determined to prove—to himself—that his view was justified. He seemed to be waiting to tell himself, "See, she is not really my friend." Unfortunately, the kids couldn't understand all that, so they fell in the trap. When he hurt them—kicked them or took their homework and ripped it in half, or teased them—he got exactly the reaction he thought he was going to get. Kids would say, "I hate you. You're mean." With me he didn't get the reaction he was looking for, and after several months things got a lot better. Not that Tony ever became an angel, but his behavior really improved, and together we could concentrate on academics.

DR. BRODKIN COMMENTS

It was so fortunate for this child that his parents and teacher trusted each other and worked together comfortably. The outlook for a child in such a situation is infinitely better than it would be if there were mutual mistrust or avoidance. It's been said before, but it's worth saying again: Any time you can work together with parents, you'll be ahead of the game. Try to find something positive about the child you can both agree on, and build from there.

There are many reasons to avoid negative reinforcement or negative discipline whenever possible. For one thing, it provides the child with your attention. Being linked with any kind of attention is likely to strengthen, rather than weaken, problematic behavior. Often, too, negative discipline doesn't help children learn what we're trying to teach them. Instead, they conclude, "Since I'm enduring the punishment and my teacher's disapproval, I'm paying my dues. So now we're even." In other words, to the child it's back to square one. The episode is over; nothing is learned and nothing is changed.

Of course, realistically, it's impossible to avoid negative discipline entirely. We can't just let unacceptable behavior go on without reacting to it. The solution may be to structure situations so that the child receives far more attention and rewards for understanding and complying with rules. Try making privileges contingent on compliance, rather than waiting to take desired things away for non-compliance. Making this happen can be quite challenging with an impulsive child, as we discover in the teacher's description below.

WORKING WITH A CHILD WHO IS OUT OF CONTROL

One of my students, Austin, was constantly disruptive. When he would go to the bathroom and come back, he was not able simply to walk to his seat. Instead, he'd run, slide, twirl, and then fall on the floor before he sat down. At the beginning of the year, the kids would laugh, but soon they began to get annoyed. They actually started to come to me and say things like, "Austin made so much noise during math that I didn't understand what you were saying." That is when I knew I had to take some action. I would sit near him during the lesson and put my arm or hand on his shoulder to let him know that I was there. That helped a lot. Or when we were sitting on the rug, I would whisper, "Austin, why don't you come sit next to me. I'd really like you to sit next to me." Then I could just put my arm out and touch his shoulder, and that would calm him down if he began to get disruptive. At the same time, I tried to call on him as much as I could because it kept him focused on the lesson. That is a tough choice, though, because I felt as if I was taking time and attention away from the others.

Here's a common dilemma with no universal solution. Once again, in each situation, the costs and benefits of a particular intervention must be considered. Maybe this teacher still felt that enabling this particular child to become a better colleague in the classroom was worth the risk of temporarily seeming to favor him over others. One thing is certain: Her reflectiveness and acute awareness of the issues bode well for all the children in her classroom.

Unfortunately, Austin had a very stressful home life; his father was an alcoholic and his mother was working two jobs. His homework was almost never done. He had been in the Resource Room, but his parents had had him removed because they thought he didn't need it. They were wrong—he did. I told them that it was their decision, but if he was in my room full time, I wouldn't be able to give him the same kind of undivided academic attention as he would get in the Resource Room. They told me that was fine, but when he started to fail that wasn't fine at all. I invited them in to observe our class and to talk, which helped a little.

Six months later—six months of lost time—Austin's parents allowed him to go back to the Resource Room. By then I was completely burned out, because although I had said that I wasn't going to give him extra help, I had, and I was acutely aware that he needed even more. He needed the Resource Room to overcome his defeatist outlook and raise his academic expectations.

> ### Dr. Brodkin comments
>
> A Resource Room can be very helpful for many children with behavior or learning challenges. In fact, any arrangement that individualizes each child's learning situation is likely to be helpful. In the classroom itself, that might translate to smaller learning groups and/or the use of an aide paired with the child in question. In any case, the opportunity for the teacher and child to become partners in an effort to enhance the child's readiness to learn is always a boon.

At their doctor's suggestion, his parents agreed to put Austin on medication. Although I don't think medication is right for all children, apparently it was for him. Before the medication he had been out of control. I don't think he wanted to be; in fact, he knew he was high-strung and was always very sorry when we were disappointed in his behavior. That didn't change the fact that two minutes later he would be doing the same disruptive thing again. His lack of self-control consistently got him in serious trouble. However, once he was back in the Resource Room and on the pediatrician's regimen, we were able to talk to him about his behavior, and he could internalize more of our suggestions.

The issue of whether and when to use medication is an extremely complex one. Fortunately, it was not the teacher's decision to make. But let's consider the complexity. It's impossible to say how much of his then current problematic behavior began with this boy's innate temperament, how much is attributable to his life circumstances and social-emotional environment, or to what extent it is a product of the way nature and nurture have interacted. It's also important to ask whether the medication was prescribed for problems that were connected to the boy's chaotic home life or to meet his actual biochemical needs.

Since, in this case, it doesn't seem that anyone is attending to the child's family environment (the father's alcoholism, the mother's stressful life), medication and the teacher's best efforts are all that is available. Does that justify the use of the medication? Some experts would say more should be done to understand the role of environmental stresses on the boy. The family could be referred to an agency whose experts are equipped to study such family struggles and to intervene with individual and/or family counseling. If these efforts are successful and chaos begins to be replaced by calm, and the boy is still struggling, he should be evaluated by a team of experts including a developmental pediatrician, a pediatric psychologist, and a child psychiatrist. If that team agrees that the boy (rather than the environment alone) needs treatment, and that an appropriate part of that treatment is medication, the prescription would be offered.

Although Austin, the child in the last example, had definite environmental issues to contend with, that is not the case with every child who doesn't conform to classroom behavioral expectations. As you will see in the next example, normal variations in temperament can be a factor.

BALANCING FREEDOM AND STRUCTURE

I had one student who was a very happy kid with no real issues at home; he just liked to talk and, in general, do whatever he wanted to do. He didn't set out to create the kinds of disruptions he caused. In other words, his effect wasn't deliberate, but I found myself constantly asking him to be quiet or putting my hand on his shoulder to try to slow him down.

These methods of intervening had obvious limitations. When he was on the other side of the room I couldn't always get to him. And sometimes with a class full of children, you just don't know whose shoulder you should put your hand on first! So I tried singling out other kids who were doing a good job, hoping that he would see what they were doing and realize that that was what I wanted him to do, too. I do hate singling children out, saying things like, "Look how nicely so-and-so is doing." But it worked with this child. In fact, to my surprise, I have found many children who respond positively to this technique. However, there wasn't much long-term change in this child. Everything I tried worked for a while, but not long enough to celebrate a true change in him.

There is something else I want to add. I don't have the kind of structured classroom setup where children sit in rows and don't move around without permission. So, I wonder if some of the behavior problems I see from time to time are my fault. Perhaps by allowing a bit of freedom, I offer an environment that some kids just can't handle, but I like children to feel free to move around. I think it's important for them to have that freedom. This child, however, crossed the boundaries of even a relaxed classroom's behavioral expectations. Every single time that things weren't structured, he would act up, as if he couldn't resist the temptation to be the center of attention.

DR. BRODKIN COMMENTS

This teacher faces an age-old dilemma: How can we allow those children who thrive in an open learning environment to have it, without leaving those who need more structure in the lurch? Once again, there is no universal solution; this means classroom situations need to be assessed each academic year. Sometimes there are only one or two children who can't handle a lack of structure. At other times you might have a class in which many children just aren't ready for a good deal of freedom. Let's look at both scenarios:

If every child but this one is thriving, it might make sense to structure one child's day differently (a resource room or other small-group setup with a well-structured learning situation or an aide who can work with him or her within the classroom). If these options aren't possible, the teacher might talk with the child and explain that until that child can function comfortably and successfully with more freedom, the rules for that child will be different from those of children who can. During their talk, she can point out that everyone else is doing okay with the present arrangement, and ask: "What can you and I do together to make this work for you?" In other words, make the child a partner in solving the problem.

Another option is to break down the steps needed to establish and maintain a smoothly running environment—even if only one student is causing the problem—and then create a class contract that spells out behavioral expectations for everyone without pointing any fingers. If this is something you'd like to try, decide what your behavioral expectations are and the consequences of meeting or not meeting them. Indicate clearly to children: "If you do this, then that will happen (or not happen)."

▷

If a significant number of children need more structure, you might be better off tightening the reins for everyone—at least for the early part of the year. As time goes on, more children will be able to ease into a less-structured environment. The point is, when kids don't have good self-control, it's certainly appropriate for a teacher to step in and modify the classroom environment in a way that may not seem consistent with the philosophy of that teacher. We all know that no two groups are identical. Last year, freedom may have reigned with ease; this year that may not be so. It's not only fine, but wise, to adapt your expectations to the situation at hand and grow, as a group, from there.

Considering a particular group's needs can be very helpful, but as we see, once again, in the next vignette, an individual child's behavior goes a long way toward explaining her social difficulties.

HELPING STUDENTS ACHIEVE SOCIAL SUCCESS

I had a child, a nice little girl whose parents were very supportive, but she was immature and did things to alienate other people. In fact, she brought a lot of problems on herself. For instance, we might be doing a group problem-solving activity and when I'd pass out materials for the whole group to use, she would just grab them all and say, "I'm gonna do it!" Or, she might be in line and see somebody cutting into the line five people behind her. Although it actually had no effect on her, she'd yell out that the person had taken cuts. Her observation would be accurate but would bring her a lot of ill will. So I'd take her aside and say, "Dara, when you did that, how do you think it made that person feel? Do you think doing that is going to help you to have more friends, or make you lose friends?"

I talked with her parents about it, and they said they were seeing the same thing at home. I explained that I was trying to bring Dara's behavior to her own attention, because so far she couldn't understand why the other children considered her very self-centered. I remember times at recess when she'd come up to me and tell me that she didn't have any friends. That is when I'd have the best chance to talk to her: "You're saying that you don't have any friends and nobody wants to play with you, but can you think of anything you might be doing that could explain that?"

Sometimes she could give me an answer, but sometimes I'd have to help by giving her an example: "You know there was something that happened today when everyone was lining up that made it so maybe someone wouldn't want to be your friend. Do you remember what it was?" But whenever that kind of opportunity arose, I'd try to help her to see something positive she had done. "You know, Dara, at lunchtime when you asked people to help go get the lunch baskets, you made them pretty happy." So I tried not to focus only on what she did wrong. In fact, I rejoiced at any chance to point out that she did some kind and wise things.

I'd also try arranging things to help her avoid rejection. For instance, if I knew the kids were going to pick partners, I'd make sure to give her one of the first chances to pick, even though some of the kids would put their hands down so she wouldn't pick them. (That's the kind of thing I'd talk with the whole class about later. I wouldn't use Dara as an example; I'd just say to everyone: "When people pick you as a partner, they're doing that for a reason—because they want to work with you. That doesn't mean you have to be best friends. It just means that person thinks you'd be a good partner. So you should feel special no matter who picks you, because getting picked is an honor." That works pretty well with first graders.)

I know that it is important to make sure that children don't feel left out. With Dara it was pretty easy to tell when rejection was about to happen; rather than ignore it, I'd bring it to her attention. When I noticed that she didn't want to hear what I had to say, I began to wonder if she knew what she was doing and was, perhaps, provoking rejection as a protective barrier early on. Maybe she felt that if other children saw her as an enemy right from the start, she wouldn't have to experience the loss of a supposed friend later on.

I don't want to overanalyze the situation. It was clear that Dara was often ambivalent, so I would just try as much as possible to keep her from feeling isolated. If there was a learning situation where I needed to have three in each group, and it was clear to me that Dara was likely to be left out in the cold, I'd set her up with a group that I knew would work well. I learned quickly that if I didn't protect her in ways like this, she'd wind up by herself, feeling defeated. In other words, I tried to make things better for her, first, by pointing out to her which behaviors do and which do not win friends, and second, by averting social defeats before they happened.

DR. BRODKIN COMMENTS

What this teacher did was remarkable. He addressed this challenge from two vantage points—the child's and that of the world around her. He did everything he could to help the girl improve things by pointing out her problematic behavior and by supporting her pro-social behavior. At the same time he cleared a path for her efforts to succeed by shielding her from possible rejection (of course, without her knowing he was doing the latter).

Dara's self-defeating behavior was certainly daunting, but it can be even tougher for a teacher to keep things calm in a situation like the one described below, in which a child is consumed with anger.

WORKING WITH ANGER

From the beginning of the year, Tyler was sitting on a stockpile of anger that he had a lot of trouble controlling. Even if someone only accidentally knocked against his chair, he would yell and act very, very angry. You could see it in his body language and his face. He was angry at everybody and everything, acting immediately and thinking later. At times I saw some remorse, so I felt there was something there to work with. I soon learned that I couldn't say anything to him in front of the class, so I would talk to him privately. First I had to talk to him about "anger busters." I generally did this with the whole class, but I found I had to work with him individually, as well. Let me explain.

In my class we talk a lot about many ways to de-stress. We also have a little list in the room that I call "Anger Busters." It includes things you can do when you get mad—count to ten, take three deep breaths, remove yourself from the situation, among others.

Tyler and I worked together and made up some private signals: a wink, a certain facial expression, a scratch on the nose. (I've used this strategy with several kids before.) The signal is a secret reminder: "I need to calm down. I need to do something to stop this explosion from happening." It usually works, and it is a way for the child to save face. (Plus, the kids usually love the intrigue.)

We used all of these methods over about six or seven months, and Tyler gradually began to feel and act better. As is the case with many students, however, it was important to involve Tyler's family. Early on, when I had begun to send notes home and the principal started to call, Tyler's stepfather came in for several conferences. He listened and agreed with me about Tyler's behavior, and I shared the tips that I was using successfully. Luckily, we had gotten together in time; Tyler soon responded positively at home to methods that had succeeded in school. In fact, later that year when we had the opportunity to write a recommendation for one kid in our class who had really improved, either in behavior or academics, I wrote about Tyler. He deservedly won the Title One award.

Looking back, this wasn't an easy process. In fact, it probably took me a good month just to see what was going on and to begin to think about what might work best. After that, there were probably two or three more months of conferring with colleagues and school guidance staff, as well as the long-term, one-on-one effort of Tyler and me working together, before things finally started to turn around. I think that happened when Tyler came to trust me, because he realized I was on his side.

In the process, I learned that Tyler had had a really tough life. He'd been taken away from his mother a number of times. (I don't know why, but presumably she was deemed unfit to care for him.) I found out that when he came to my class, he was very stressed and angry because he was expecting to be sent back to her soon. This was not an easy situation. So it was even more important to help him learn to control his temper. I also wanted to help him use his energies to solve problems, to focus, and to know whom to call and where to go if things with his mother should get out of hand. Nowadays he still slips up occasionally, but all I have to do is look at him and say, "Tyler, think about what you're doing," and he calms down. He's a really good success story.

Dealing with Anger

Learning to accept and manage anger is one of life's great challenges, and it all begins in childhood. We hope that children will find the delicate balance between being out of control with rage and overcontrolling their anger. Anger is, after all, a normal human emotion, which should be accepted as long as no one gets hurt and no property is destroyed. Never or rarely expressing anger can evoke anxiety and somatic distress, not to mention the depletion of energy necessary to learn. As guiding adults, we should listen respectfully to children's expression of angry feelings. From their point of view, they are justified in proclaiming that something isn't fair. What's more, it's important to note that all anger doesn't have to result in negative behavior. The same aggressive energy that fuels angry outbursts can be converted to positive use, supporting the drive toward many kinds of mastery. Children's and adults' determination to explore, to develop skills, to take positive risks, to work toward achieving many accomplishments, is energized by a well of positive aggression. So, as you work with children, keep in mind that:

🌸 It's important for children to know that it's okay to feel angry but not okay to allow their anger to explode.

🌸 Anger isn't a *bad* emotion. Everyone feels angry at one time or another. It is important to strive to understand why anger is there.

🌸 There are many different reasons children feel angry: tension at home, disappointment, frustration, feeling cornered or attacked emotionally, to name a few. As with adults, a variety of situations and personal circumstances can cause children to feel this way.

🌸 One strategy is to try to empathize with a child's feelings and wishes and show that empathy, then point out the parameters of the situation. At the same time you can bring a broader perspective and a calmness to the situation that may enable the child to think more clearly.

🌸 Keep in mind that many so-called negative feelings—anger, jealousy, and the like—can generate energy and a sense of purpose. Dr. Stanley Greenspan explains in his book *The Challenging Child* (Addison Wesley, 1995—Chapter 7, pp. 236–238) that this doesn't mean that "...a lot of rage and competition is helpful; they can overload children. But against a background of warmth, love, empathy, and acceptance, there is nothing like a little bit of anger or jealousy to get the motor going!"

🌸 To paraphrase Dr. Greenspan, by helping children acknowledge the full range of their feelings, including anger, we can help them grow into integrated human beings who are capable of being both competitive and nurturing.

Children who feel supported can get comfortable with a broad range of feelings, yet still make appropriate choices about how to behave. The next teacher's comment illustrates how support can build a child's confidence. Supporting children and assuring them we believe in them is vital for our goals, since many children who disrupt do not believe in themselves.

BUILDING SELF-CONFIDENCE IS KEY

Last year I had a child, Nate, in my kindergarten. He had been retained. His teacher had asked me if I would take him because she thought my room would be good for him. I said sure, but asked her to tell me about him. She explained, "He has a very negative stance. He doesn't listen. He's argumentative. He has no self-control. And he's immature." I already knew that this particular teacher tended to say things like this all the time, so I didn't overreact. In fact, there were times when this teacher thought that any kid who was active was a problem. Then she asked me to meet with the parent because the parent wanted to meet with me.

Nate's mother came in and said that her son had had a terrible year, that his teacher had disliked him and he knew it, and his self-esteem had really suffered. She was at her wits' end and felt sure that he needed another year of kindergarten. I made up my mind during that conference that no matter what his behavior was like, I wasn't going to have a child in my room who felt bad about himself all year.

And that was how we started. When Nate came to my room, he had a lot of difficulty controlling himself. He blurted out whatever he wanted, he interrupted, and he was pushy. Trying to control situations with adults and his peers, he would tell everybody what to do. His social skills were immature, but he had a certain sophistication. This may have come from his older brother, although I think the brother may have used Nate as a punching bag. I got the feeling that Nate was trying to compensate for this by being the big man on his turf away from home: his classroom. I wanted to give him the chance to be a big man, but not in a way that was problematic for everybody else.

I found out that Nate had traveled a lot with his parents. During class discussions and during our writer's workshop, which we have every day, I encouraged Nate to talk and write about his travels. We came to look upon him as our travel expert, and I tried to make sure that whenever possible he had the opportunity to share a story or an anecdote. Empowering him in that way made it possible for me to have discussions with him about controlling his blurting out and interrupting other children. He was able to understand that, just as it was important for him to tell his stories and important for him to know other children were listening and valuing what he was saying, it was also important for him to give everyone else the same respect.

It sounds simple, but it was really hard for him, really hard. We tried several strategies until one worked. We decided that when Nate wanted to say something, he had to raise his hand and count to three in his head before he said it. At first he learned to raise his hand, but he would blurt out whatever he wanted to say at the same time. It really helped when I asked him to put one finger on his lips and raise his other hand at the same time. That was the beginning of a major change in his behavior. A rather experimental start proved to be just what Nate needed. By picking up on his strength and helping him turn it into an asset, I was able to help Nate gain enough self-confidence to recognize and work on some adverse behaviors he had developed. From then on he began to move into a new place in the class as well as in his own mind.

Building on Strengths

Discovering and then building on an individual's strengths is both a caring and psychologically sound technique used by many successful teachers, parents, and therapists. For some who are emotionally gifted, like the teacher above, it is intuitive. Others of us have had to learn to bolster strengths and earn trust before asking someone to change. Here are a few hints about what you might try:

- If you are having difficulty with a particular student, try to step back and observe her as if you've never seen her before. Or ask a colleague to come in to help you with this process.

- Jot down as many positive qualities or strengths as you can. (You may need to find out more about the child: her interests, experiences, and so on. This information may provide you with insights on which to build.)

- Note a few behaviors you wish could change. Concentrate on only rewarding the positive for a day or two.

- Stop and reflect again: Are you making any headway? Are you seeing her in a better light? Has anything changed in your relationship? Is she surprised to find out that someone recognizes something good in her?

- Keep the positive reinforcement going as long as you can, then choose one of the behaviors you're hoping you can change, and ask her to work together with you.

After his previous year of failure, I was determined to discover what might help Nate feel special, this time in a positive sense. An opportunity appeared in a most unlikely place. In my class we meet on the rug in the mornings. There happened to be one chair beside the one where I sit, which many children always ran to sit in. Sometimes I would say, "No chairs," because I didn't want to have a battle, but there were days when I was inconsistent and a child ended up sitting there. I noticed that when Nate got to the chair first, he was really good at controlling himself. So I started, on purpose, to ignore the fact that he was soon sitting in the chair almost every day. It helped that none of the other kids said anything either. I decided it helped Nate feel like he had a special privilege, because he seemed to draw that conclusion. Here was an important opportunity to counter his experience the year before, when he didn't trust his teacher, and he felt pretty crummy every day.

Nate didn't talk about the year before, but I noticed that when I talked to him in a way he must have perceived as different from that of his teacher last year, he would get a look of surprise on his face. I felt like I could read his thoughts: "This teacher is really funny," or, "Hey, she thinks I'm funny and we're having fun together!"

Nate is also a fabulous artist. At the beginning of the school year, we began our Writer's Workshop. We did this every day, and in a very short time, writing became a very big thing in our class. One day Nate made a beautiful picture of the group and wrote at the top: "The Writer's Workshop Club." This elicited a wonderful feeling, among all of us, just what I had wished for—a community of writers who were also kids, writing together. It was a huge picture. Every day all of us made such a big deal about it. It was so celebrated, not just the picture, but the feeling behind it. And so we became known as the Writer's Workshop Club Class. This gave Nate a tremendous boost and position. Not to say that there weren't days when he was more difficult than others, but I think the experiences at the beginning of the year helped him help himself get better at what he needed to do to function in the classroom in a positive way.

Nothing's ever simple, however. Nate still had control issues. I remember around Valentine's Day we were graphing candy hearts by color. I gave each child ten candy hearts to graph, and suddenly I noticed Nate getting up and walking around to every group, counting to make sure everybody had the same number of hearts. I said, "Nate, don't you trust me? I said I was going to give everybody ten and I really did." He replied, " Just wanted to make sure." At his age, most kids just assume the adult is being straight with them, but not Nate. He did that kind of thing during any game. He was really on the lookout for cheating and would cry cheating often when he had really just misunderstood someone else's actions.

Nate talked a lot about getting beat up by his brother and his brother getting in trouble for it. When I spoke to his mother, she didn't want any advice from me. And since I learned early on that I can't control what happens at home but I can control my classroom environment, I hoped that maybe Nate could make some changes in school that would spill over to home. Over time I was able to see that he felt better when he did something good. I think he had felt that there wasn't much that was really good about him. Now he knows he has many skills and talents, and he uses them on a daily basis.

My hope for Nate is that he will start next year with a positive feeling about his teacher and about coming to school. I hope that he will retain a positive feeling about himself and about his ability to be in control. With time, hopefully, he will feel empowered to make choices about his behavior to achieve what he wants interpersonally and academically at nobody else's expense.

DR. BRODKIN COMMENTS

If at all possible, it is vital to work with the parents of kids who have problematic behavior. When, for a variety of reasons, that isn't possible, teachers may achieve much by making their classrooms an oasis of reasonable, considerate, caring behavior in a child's otherwise chaotic world. The tough part is knowing when "to settle" for that, hoping that the positive classroom experience will dilute the power of the troubles in a child's life. Think of the Alcoholics Anonymous prayer: "Help me to have the strength to change the things I can change, accept those that I can't change, and the wisdom to know the difference."

The next three stories show how three different teachers reached out to parents, making every effort to change the things they could.

BUILDING BRIDGES: SCHOOL TO HOME

Dylan was a child who made himself known in our school right away. He was very loud, called out of turn, poked other people, and needed a lot of recognition. Dylan had been poking people a lot, and some children came to talk to me about it. I had seen him do it, so I could verify their complaints. Dylan and I talked it over. Often that does the trick, but in Dylan's case, it did not. There was no change. The next step would be to phone his mother. I rarely get to this point, but when I do, this is how I handle it. I explain to the child that he and I are going to make the call together from school. In this situation, I asked Dylan to dial the number and assure his mom that everything was okay, and then hand the phone to me. I got on and introduced myself, and calmly related what the call was about. "Dylan is fine; he's right here, and he's going to tell you more about why we are calling." I prefer that the child speak for himself, but in my presence. Dylan told his mom what he had done on the playground, whom he had pushed, and that he'd poked some kids in the room. (At this point, like most children, Dylan listened quietly to what his parent was saying.) I took the phone again, and asked Dylan's mom if she would have time to talk with me about our mutual concern. Dylan's mother was very concerned because, as she said, that is not the sort of behavior she and her husband want to see or hear about.

I had often observed Dylan's mom with her children at school, so I knew that setting limits was difficult for her. On the phone, however, she said that they would talk this over as a family and come up with a plan. In the morning, Dylan did indeed bring a written plan to school. It suggested a reduction of TV time and some chores for Dylan—a kind of community service at home. I was to send a note home at the end of each day relating how Dylan had behaved, and he would add a message in his own handwriting. His parent would read the report, sign it, and send it back. At that point we began ongoing accountability with Dylan very much involved. It was the beginning of a real breakthrough.

Strategies to Help Children Control Impulses

✿ Acknowledge the problem. For example, Dylan's teacher said to him: "Dylan, it's great that you know how to behave in this room, but sometimes you don't seem to know how to behave in other places like the playground, the halls, and on the bus."

✿ Talk with the child. Reflect together on successful behavior strategies the child is already using. For example, the child may say, "I'm good at waiting for other people to have a turn," or, "It doesn't bother me when someone cuts in front of me in line." See if you can help the child apply the same or similar strategies in different situations.

✿ Help children find language to describe their choices of behavior.

✿ Consider that expectations at home may be different from those at school. Help children understand what is expected of them in your class and how they can meet those expectations.

✿ If possible, involve families, so children can feel encouraged in and out of school.

✿ Above all, consider individual needs. For instance, one child might respond to a behavior contract where you set the expectations together. (See "Writing Effective Contracts" on page 27.) Another child may need you to sit down one-on-one, and go over the class rules together. Still another child may need to think about where he or she could sit to increase the probability of positive behavior.

✿ Observe. Take time to see if there is a problem between children. Then, sit down together and ask each child to explain his or her position. Next, restate what all three of you heard. Then, ask children to come up with a solution, establish a plan together, and help them follow through. (Stay close by so you can support any change in behavior.)

✿ When you speak to a child once about a specific undesirable behavior, make it clear that if he or she chooses to repeat that behavior, there will be a consequence.

I got to know George when I taught his older brother, Sam, who had cerebral palsy. George had been a preschooler who would come to my room to visit. He grew up with the knowledge that his brother had a physical difference from other people. His dad accepted that fact more calmly than his mother did. I could tell Sam evoked unwelcome feelings in her; she was anxious and impatient with him. The reason I'm sharing this is that all of it affected George. Although his physical health was fine, a good part of the behavior he adopted reflected the way he interacted in his family as the "well-bodied child." He brought to school a restlessness, a need to shout out, and a strong need to be recognized. This was evident in many ways, including his calling attention to his physical strength and all the feats he could accomplish on the playground. Because I knew the family background, I was sensitive to George's messages, and over time I was able to gain his mom's trust. I explained to her that I felt every parent of a child with special needs is entitled to counseling, and as she got help she began to recognize George's own special needs. Together we were able to help him recognize that he didn't have to carry the strong male mantle for the next generation of his family. He just needed to be really good at being George. That meant there would be some areas of academics and sports in which he wouldn't perform at the absolute top, and some where he would have his share of successes. It was gratifying, but hard work, to help both George and his mom learn how to accept the big picture of what it means to be a "normal boy," which includes having both strengths and frailties.

An important part of this effort was helping George recognize and verbalize the strengths of others. When he would come in from recess, I would ask him to name someone he had noticed doing something nice for someone else or speaking kindly to another person. It took some work, some coaxing and reminders, but as George grew in his ability to accept himself, this strategy seemed to help him accept others realistically as well. That all happened in the first grade. Now George is in fourth grade and he is well-regarded by his peers. With his mom's help, the burden seems to have been lifted from him—he no longer has to be the center of attention, nor does he have to be perfect. His brother, Sam, has had some corrective surgery, but his body is still not fully functioning. He has some real talents, too, and both boys are regarded more as individuals with their own needs and strengths by their parents. Hindsight, in this case, is very gratifying and makes what was a tough process very worthwhile.

DR. BRODKIN COMMENTS

Often one of the toughest tasks that falls to teachers is referring children or their family members for counseling. Understandably, teachers are concerned about parents misinterpreting the suggestion, hearing it as an implicit criticism of their parenting or even of their own mental health. Once again, every situation is different. I find that often, once there has been a positive relationship established, such concerns can be allayed by saying, "I think anyone who is dealing with the kinds of things you're facing is entitled to counseling," or "entitled to have a place of her own to talk things over." One may then consider following this respectful observation with a personal example, such as, "When my brother was going through a divorce, we encouraged him (one might even say, gave him permission) to see a counselor, and according to him, it made all the difference in the world."

HELPING CHILDREN SET AND MEET PERSONAL GOALS

Adrian's records said he was a behavior problem because he wanted to be in control of everything. He didn't want to play with other kids if he couldn't be the boss; he wouldn't cooperate. However, I thought he was a little boy who had great leadership potential.

I knew he was an only child, so he didn't have to share or cooperate with other kids at home. His parents were from Romania, and he spoke fluent Romanian and excellent English. He was very bright, and I thought he had many great things going for him—he was organized, creative, and he wanted to please adults. He was the only kid in my class who was reading unabridged classics, because his parents had encouraged him to do that. But he had a real problem working with other kids. When I talked to his mom, my first suggestion involved getting him to be part of some kind of team sport, where he would learn to cooperate in order to win.

Interestingly, from the very beginning, I could easily talk to Adrian. What's more, he listened. So I had a little personal conference with him. I told him what I wanted him to work on; I just laid it out in clear terms. We talked about what his goals would be, and then we listed on paper how he would be able to attain them. One goal we agreed on was being able to work cooperatively. I could tell from our conversation that this concept was quite new to him, so I gave him very specific, concrete directions: "I want you to work in a team during Social Studies. That means listening to the other children, thinking about their ideas, taking turns, and offering your ideas but not being too pushy or insistent that things be done your way. I think you can do it." I asked him if he knew why I thought so. He answered unselfconsciously, "Because I'm smart. I'm organized. I have good ideas."

Together we made a contract, acknowledging everything he was working toward, including recognizing and reporting his successes. One day soon after that, he came up to me and said, "Yesterday when we had a field trip you had to switch me to another group at the last minute, and I wasn't with the person I wanted to be with, and I didn't even cry." (The week before he had made a fuss when he was separated from a particular boy, and he knew that part of his contract was to become more flexible.) So we wrote that example down as a real sign of success—he had recognized this change in his behavior and reported it to me.

All the children in my room know that when anyone meets an academic or behavioral challenge that person has set, then he or she gets to go to lunch with me. Everyone also knows that personal challenges are confidential; I am the only one who knows them. As children work on their challenges, part of the agreement is that they have to come to me at the end of the day and say, "This is what I did today in working toward my goal." When I see that their behavior has grown into a new good habit, that's when we go to lunch. In time, Adrian met his goal of becoming cooperative with his peers. When I informed him, he said he would like to wait until his friend met his challenge too, so the three of us could go to lunch together. The process had worked and it kept on working. As the year went on, it was undeniable that Adrian really had learned to cooperate and share.

Writing Effective Contracts

Writing individual contracts is an art. It takes:

- Getting to know the child.

- Flexibility and vision to tailor each contract to that particular teacher-child partnership. (Make sure the number of goals you decide on isn't too overwhelming to achieve.)

- Helping the child strive for a "Goldilocks reach," not too far to be achieved and not too close to lose the meaning of true accomplishment.

- Variety. No contract is forever, or even necessarily for a semester or a week. In some cases you might design a new contract at the end of each day for the next day—whatever the situation calls for.

- Freedom to experiment and individualize.

Contracts are as effective as their sensitivity to each particular child, teacher, and classroom setting. Gradual success with children who are disruptive will be aided by making behavior expectations very clear at the outset, since many of these children have not previously been introduced to a clear and consistent definition of the boundaries of acceptable behavior. The next step is to take your time getting to know each child—be a keen observer, searching for the child's strengths and interests, as well as the setting and circumstances of his or her loss of control. Call on others whom you trust—school staff, including child-study team members, administrators, and colleagues—to share their observations and advice. Then design a plan of intervention based on everything you've learned. Trust your hunches about what may help turn things around. Often you may find it useful to enlist the support of the class as a whole in carrying out your plan. But your most effective ally in creating positive change will be the child himself or herself. Plan your strategy together, and be sure to communicate your faith, while you also define clear and consistent behavioral consequences, emphasizing predominantly positive rewards.

Children Who Turn Inward

All too often, the "too quiet child" may be overlooked in a busy classroom. That is most unfortunate, since many children who turn inward are suffering silently, and may go on to miss out on many of life's rewards as adults—and the world misses out on the contributions they might have made. The teachers we interviewed felt this very keenly, and, as you will see in the vignettes below, they were determined to make their classrooms a "safe place" for inhibited children to risk emerging from obscurity.

DRAWING CHILDREN OUT

Sometimes you have a quiet child as a student, someone who may barely tune in to classroom matters. I had two such children last year and found that to draw them out, I had to touch base with each one as much as possible, to acknowledge them regularly, to let them know I saw them as valuable individuals, and to help them believe that I cared. One of these students, Gabrielle, was really struggling. She just didn't have any confidence in her own abilities. My strategy was to find things that she was good at, so that we could build on them together. I asked myself what her talents were and talked to her about her hobbies. The next step was to figure out how we could bring those unique assets into the classroom. Eventually, I found out that this child loved nonfiction. (It took a little while to discover this because I didn't expect reading to be the key. Gabrielle was one of my low-level readers.) But once I did, I worked hard to find high-interest books at her reading level and offered them to her regularly.

Another internalizing child, Max, was in a similar situation. I talked to his parents and let them know my concern: The more a child tunes out, the less likely he is to begin to do the work; it takes a greater and greater effort as time goes by. Sometimes parents are just as frustrated and eager to intervene as I am. They are often ready to create a plan together and follow through on it. That wasn't the case with Max's parents. They insisted he was different at home—completely fine. That may have been the case, because his interests and activities were so different outside of school—he loved being outdoors, hiking, and fishing with family members. But something had to be done for him in school. He knew he was often missing the point in class, and he was starting to doubt his own abilities. The more I observed, the more I saw a child who was unsure of what to do and how to do it, even when he was sufficiently engaged to try. Max was caught up in a terrible cycle.

It was clear that, for now at least, I had to handle this entirely within the classroom, so I moved his seat and placed him right in front of me so I could tell when he was tuning out. I also asked my aide to stay near him during work time to make sure he completely understood what was expected of him. It was tough, really tough—especially because this particular kid didn't fit in with the other kids in class. (He had one good friend who was in another class.) We helped him to a point, but not enough. It was very frustrating, especially since he was one of those kids who you know has talent; you know it's in there, but it's just so hard to pull out.

> ### DR. BRODKIN COMMENTS
>
> This teacher describes an uphill battle to rescue a child who turns inward. It is difficult to do without parental cooperation and without supportive peers, so it's a tribute to the teacher's determination and confidence in the boy that he did make progress. The teacher may not realize just how much progress he has made or how vital her faith in him has been. Sometimes faith, intuition, gut feelings, and a lot of patience are all that we have to rely on. In the teacher's story that follows, these ingredients prove to be essential.

HELPING CHILDREN EXPRESS THEMSELVES

I had a little girl who was shut down, and it really killed me. She didn't bother anybody. She was the kind of person you always hear about, the kind of child who falls through the cracks because she doesn't make any noise. I couldn't tell what this child was thinking. All I knew was that she seemed to be somewhere else.

Her name was Stephanie, and for the most part, she preferred to sit off to the side. Sometimes she looked blank, and sometimes she looked like she was listening, but she really wasn't. When I asked her questions, she'd respond, "I didn't raise my hand," or, "Can you come back to me?" (These are options I give children when it seems like they need more time to think.) Or sometimes she'd just say, "I don't know." I told her that it was her job to do some thinking and it was my job to help. She seemed to understand this, but didn't buy in to it. She never would participate in Show and Tell. She just said that she forgot to bring anything. And she seemed so fragile that I didn't want to push it.

Her mother said, in the beginning of the year, that her daughter was shy and very quiet at home. She was an only child who didn't speak a lot in front of adults. I sensed, though, that she had a rich fantasy world. One day I observed her when she didn't know it, and I was surprised to see just how social she was with the kids. In fact, in the after-school center she was really loud, a different child in that different role, out of her shell. I had never seen such contrast in a child's behavior before. And then one day, at rest time, I noticed her talking to a pretend person about things in the classroom, with a very different voice and a very energetic light in her eyes. It was so odd.

Most of the time she was almost angelic, with a persona that appeared so perfect. But I sensed that underneath there was a robust individual who was scared to come out too publicly. I also had glimpses of that person when she was truly wild on the playground or in dramatic play. In fact, it made me wonder if she felt she had to be perfect in class, and because she couldn't, she simply shut down.

Stephanie didn't seem to have confidence in her ideas, or maybe she felt she had no right to have ideas, and as a result, she stopped generating any. As my usual practice dictates, I tried to find those unexpressed good ideas—they don't have to be *great* ideas. I tried to come upon her thinking or doing something that I could acknowledge with enthusiasm. Here's an example that worked. She wrote a wonderful story about all the things she liked. It took a long while for her to do it. When it was done, we celebrated, and everyone in the class liked it. This sort of thing happened more than a few times, but the acclaim never seemed to have a lasting effect.

I got a note from her mom that said, "Don't worry. Stephanie is just like I was." That let me know that there was an open acceptance of the little girl's behavior, maybe even a positive expectation that she be "shy." I felt I had to be honest and told her mother that it was more than just being shy; it was like Stephanie's mind was somewhere else. I told this to Stephanie, too.

Finally, I talked to a child psychologist who advised me to encourage Stephanie to do as much dramatic play as she wanted—free play that would give free reign to her imagination through storytelling or story reading. The psychologist also encouraged me to communicate enthusiastically to her parents that their daughter had a wonderful imagination and was potentially quite creative, but hid these things for fear of disapproval. "Congratulate them," the psychologist said. "Help them encourage Stephanie's emotional freedom, and express her feelings through play, reading, and writing stories."

I almost wanted to hold their hands—to give them license to let Stephanie feel things, to really listen to her stories and praise them. I also told the teacher she would have the next year about this positive aspect of Stephanie—and tried to communicate that this child appeared to have two selves, one who seemed very contained and the other who had a much freer quality. I don't think I'm overstating all this, because at times she was nearly immobilized by anxiety, which blocked her from learning and doing. Often she sat and tried to write a story and then looked up and said, "I can't think." I still worry about her. Because she doesn't make much noise, she may just get lost in the shuffle of school.

DR. BRODKIN COMMENTS

This teacher has a very special gift of insight and the courage to share it with us. What is more, she follows up with valuable action on behalf of the child. The ideal next step would be to find a way to win the trust of the parents so that the little girl might feel free to be herself and ultimately have an opportunity to work with an expert in play therapy. Of course, that is so much easier said than done, and I share the teacher's frustration about a child with a potential for expressing a broad range of thoughts and feelings, who is inhibited by fear of disapproval.

This next teacher blends insight with humility and courage in order to rescue a child from socially crippling inhibition.

ONE SMALL STEP AT A TIME

I had been teaching about four years when I had a child in my class who had several years before been diagnosed as a "selective mute." That child, Jasmine, turned out to be my success story. She came to me not speaking, and she left my room carrying on ordinary conversations.

At the beginning of the year, I said to her, "Jasmine, I do expect you to communicate with me this year, although I understand that at times you have a problem with speaking in school." I gave her a set of sticky-notes and told her, "Here is the plan. I will call on you, and I expect you to write your answer on the sticky-pad, and I will read it out loud. Do you understand? Can you do this?" She kind of shrugged her shoulders, so that was all I said; I didn't want to push it. Silently, though, I thought, "We're going to make this work." She very seldom put her hand up at the beginning of the year. Eventually, as time went on, she did. She wouldn't talk, but she would raise her hand.

About mid-year I began to feel that what I was doing wasn't working well enough, because she still wasn't talking. (It is important to mention that Jasmine did talk outside of school, but not in school.) I spoke with her parents and told them I would like to take Jasmine out for a pizza, and they said fine. I told Jasmine that she could pick a friend to come along, and she picked Kelly. I'll never forget it. She wrote down her friend's name, and I said, "You talk to Kelly and I'll talk to her mother, but when I pick you up in the car, I'm going to look at you, and I'm going to say, 'Jasmine, what is your favorite kind of pizza?' and I expect you to answer me with your voice." Her eyes were as big as saucers, and I could tell she was thinking, "You're kidding!" Then I said, "If you don't, I will have to ask you to get out of the car, and unfortunately, I will have to go home. That will make me very sad." I asked her to think about it and get back to me. The next day I asked her again, and she indicated that she thought she could do it. So we set the date, and when I went to pick them up I could see her talking to Kelly in the driveway. But as soon as I pulled in, she clammed up. I said, "Hi, girls," and Kelly began talking a mile a minute. Once they were in the car, I said, "Jasmine, what is your favorite kind of pizza?" She didn't say anything. And my heart sank. So I took a deep breath, looked at her again, and said, "Jasmine, you know the deal. You need to speak to me. Just one word is enough. Then we'll go get it." I asked her again, and she said, "Pepperoni." I didn't know what to do. Finally, I was able to say, "Great, that is mine, too."

The entire evening she didn't shut up. She talked and talked and talked. I got the whole family history. Toward the end of the evening, I told her that I didn't expect her to come back to school and start talking in front of everybody, but I wanted to spend recess the next day with Kelly and her. (Kelly had already said she'd be willing to help.) So the three of us spent recess together, and we read a book, a little book. I said, "Each one of us is going to read a page." So here she was talking in school with Kelly, who I knew she was comfortable with, and me. I said that we'd do this again in two days and that she should choose another person to add to the group. She chose another girl and was a little bit nervous, so I said, "If you want to pass, just put your hand up. But before recess ends I want you to read." Of course, she passed about five or six times, and I finally said, "Okay, Jasmine, you're really going to have to do it this time." And she did!

> "What a gift it is that we teachers have—the opportunity to work with each of our children. Whether they've been joyful or challenging, they have each helped me to grow. No matter what they're like, one of the greatest things that we can do is find a way to enjoy them. They will sense that, and it will make a huge difference in their lives."
>
> —fifth-grade teacher

Every day I added a person until we had five or six kids. Jasmine still wasn't talking in front of the whole class, only in our small group at recess. So I started having her read to me during buddy reading time, when there was other noise in the room. We did that, and then she read with her reading group. Little by little she came out of her shell. The last thing I asked her to do was bring a note to another teacher and say, "This is from Mrs. Jones." She did it! We had taken the tiniest little baby steps together, compromising, letting her pass sometimes, but letting her know that I expected things from her. You know, thinking back, it would have been hard, but I would have walked away from that pizza date.

Toward the end of the year, I offered to take her to the dentist. I knew she still wasn't talking in public places, and it was a problem. I told her I just wanted her to say something. "If all you say is hello, I will feel that you've made progress." It wasn't easy. She was so nervous that on the way we had to pull over because she thought she was going to throw up. When we went in I held her hand; she was shaking like a leaf. At one point, she was so nervous that I had to ask the dentist to leave for just a bit. All I could do was try to calm her down. When the dentist came back, Jasmine spoke to him. She really did it! That's when I knew she would be okay. And she is. She had one of the leads in this year's sixth-grade play.

DR. BRODKIN COMMENTS

The zeal, optimism, courage, patience, and sensitive timing of this teacher can only be marveled at. The combination was lifesaving for the child. The teacher's words are far more inspiring than anything I might try to add. My suggestion: Reread her words when you feel discouraged.

This unconventional intervention worked for this child and this teacher, and it may even have worked better than any behavioral expert's intervention. However, I would like to state quite clearly that this is the exception and not the rule. It is not only that most teachers would not or could not find the time for extra-school things like going out for dinner with a child, but that children and families with complex difficulties are usually in need of expert professional intervention. The matter is further complicated by the fact that many such families will not follow through on getting the help they need. In other words, I urge caution, but still recognize the extraordinarily heroic, and possibly lifesaving, efforts of these particular teachers.

Thinking About Inward Children

As you strive to see the world through the eyes of each individual child, consider these insights about a child who chooses to turn inward.

- Children who turn inward tend to fall between the cracks because they make so little noise.

- A particularly quiet child may barely tune in to classroom activities. Ask yourself: Why is this child so quiet, so by himself, so uninvolved?

- Remember, the more a child tunes out, the less likely he is to begin to do the work, because getting involved takes greater effort as time goes by.

- Sometimes inward children get caught up in a cycle—unsure of what to do and how to do it even when they are willing to try.

- Discover what the child's real interests are, and begin to build a bridge to classroom experience and the people in it.

- Helping a child who turns inward is very difficult without parental cooperation.

- The steps you take to show a child you're interested—the effort you make to bridge the gap, whether it be a meeting of minds or of smiles—may positively affect the child not only this year, but for years and years to come.

Throughout this chapter, we have seen the enormous potential rewards for both child and teacher when teachers are intent on helping children whose behavior is problematic. Whether that behavior is disruptive or avoidant, the keys to change include tuning in and getting to know each child, clearly communicating an unwavering faith in him or her, being consistent yet flexible, and working with each individual in a unique way designed to meet his or her particular needs.

CHAPTER 2

CREATING AN ENVIRONMENT FOR LEARNING:
The Classroom as a Caring Community

A CLASSROOM ENVIRONMENT that is welcoming, accepting, calm, caring, and safe, a community where children enjoy success, feel understood, and respect each other, can go a long way toward influencing behavior. Of course, some children will need more intervention than others, but having a caring classroom provides a good beginning, as the teachers' stories in this section demonstrate.

SECTION ONE

Setting Up at the Beginning of the Year

THE MOST IMPORTANT TEACHING YOU DO ALL YEAR

In my classroom I strive to create an environment of caring and support, where children feel safe and can say, "I'm sad today," or "This is hard for me." This is an environment where children feel safe enough to learn.

I start off the year by saying, "This is a happy family. These are the people in your family whom you care about." Some kids don't have a sense of family, so they don't know what that means. But they see other kids modeling it, and they learn real fast what works and what doesn't.

Thinking About Praise

As you strive to encourage children through praise, consider the following suggestions:

- Keep your words and tone even and positive. Children hear more than the content of what you are saying. If your voice and/or your message conveys criticism, children may not respond. For example, "Victor, you finally remembered to bring the book back. I'm so glad," has a hostile edge to it.

- Make sure children can't construe words of praise as condescending. After all, children, like adults, respond to respect. Even the smallest child can detect mixed messages, whether you mean them or not, in statements such as, "What a good little helper you are!"

- Try not to compare children or hold one child up as the model. In your quest to appreciate each child as an individual and to help children do the same, make an effort to refrain from statements such as, "Look at Kyle. He's sitting so still during story. Let's everyone try to sit like Kyle." Instead, a more simple, "Kyle, thanks for listening while I read," will be much more effective.

- Comment on the child's accomplishment. Rather than a quick "good job," take time to notice specifics about what the child has done, or is doing.

- Don't make pronouncements. Rather than saying, "I like what you're doing," eliminate the first person and make the comment about the child: "Kelly, that's a really clever way to approach the problem. Could you tell me more about it?"

- Praise from the heart. Offering sincere words of appreciation about a polite action, a terrific joke that made the class (and you) smile, or a project completed after much effort, can be an invaluable contribution to a child's self-confidence. Don't hesitate to "reward" these gems with your own verbal excitement.

Then I talk about signals. I call them "quiet signals" and explain to children, "If someone next to you is talking, use a quiet signal to remind him or her nicely that it's work time." I also consistently give tickets and rewards to anybody who does anything nice or correct. In the beginning of the year I go through a roll of tickets in no time, because in the first two weeks, anybody who's standing in line correctly or reminds someone to stand in line correctly is rewarded. They're rewarded and rewarded and rewarded, almost to a fault. I don't do a lot of academic teaching in the first three weeks. I do more rewarding and pointing out how pleased I am with appropriate behavior. I think it's the most important teaching I do all year because it makes the rest of the year teachable.

Visitors often say, "The kids in your room are just so kind and caring; how do you do it?" And I say, "I knock myself out the first few weeks expressing kindness, and I ask the same of them." Someone's got to believe in them, in their ability to be caring. If I don't, there's no reason to believe in myself as a teacher. I see children who had been considered behaviorally hopeless transformed all the time. I've seen it happen, so I know it can happen again.

DR. BRODKIN COMMENTS

We are discovering just how powerful it can be to let a child know again and again that you believe in his or her capacity to succeed. In fact, this is a very powerful way to predict lifelong success—even among children at risk. Resilience, in the face of negative odds, is often traceable to the firm, clear faith of an important adult during childhood.

Of course, it is also important to encourage students to treat each other with kindness and respect. The next two vignettes illustrate how some teachers help to bring out these behaviors.

MOVING FROM "IT'S MINE" TO "IT'S OURS"

I set up my room more as a community than as a classroom. We have tables instead of desks. I ask children to bring in markers and pencils of a specific brand (so everyone has the same kind, and no one feels like a "have" or a "have not"). Then I take all the markers and put them in bins. There's a bin for each table, so when we do crafts no one is thinking about whose marker is whose. Everyone starts out equally; things are not "mine" or "yours," they're "ours."

SETTING A POSITIVE TONE

At the beginning of each year, I set standards of mutual respect: I will respect the children and they will respect me. I also remind myself that I am going to listen to whatever my students have to say—not just the words, but the merit of what they're feeling. I believe that conscious decision-making sets the positive tone of the room. And I try very hard to consistently model the way I want to be treated and the way I want the children to treat each other.

Of course, some things depend on the dynamics of the group. I can't say that I have a set plan, or a set day, or a set moment to do something. What happens may be the product of my intuition or someone's spontaneous remark. We may be sitting around on the floor together, and I feel I have the children's attention, and they're ready to hear things the way I want them to be heard. I know that timing is very important. If I plan ahead precisely what and when I'm going to say something, and the kids just happen to be rolling all over the rug, whatever I say is just not going to matter.

I do have a few specific rules which may influence the mood of the classroom. Some rules are for safety (no running in the classroom) while others help to support the goal of mutual respect. For kindergartners, having many rules in the beginning is just too overwhelming. They're too young, so I go for safety first. I also have a rule about always raising your hand when you want to say something, and I give them a reason. I explain that I really can't hear more than one person at a time, and I want to hear what each person wants to say. So in that first week of school we talk about only three or four rules.

DR. BRODKIN COMMENTS

While some teachers are comfortable with this approach, others, especially in upper grades, feel that clarifying expectations in a more formal way helps to set the right tone.

Five Benefits of Staying in Tune with Your Children's Moods

- You can seize the teachable moment for interpersonal as well as academic growth.

- Sensitive timing will make the big breakthroughs you've been waiting for more likely to happen.

- The only tool you need is your own sensitivity.

- You can involve children in ways that are meaningful to them, so the calm classroom becomes theirs to protect and defend.

- Children will feel more understood and will have fewer reasons to act out.

CREATING A CLASS CONTRACT

Our principal starts the year with a clear, strong expression of his philosophy by telling both parents and kids, "Our school is an educational setting. Our teachers are here to teach and provide an education. If your child is disruptive or taking away from his or her teacher's time to teach, I will intervene; disruptive behavior will not be dealt with in class time." Teachers then can say to children, "My job is to provide an education for everyone here. You may not disturb or distract other kids from learning."

In my class, on the first or second day of school, we write up a class contract. We come up with five basic rules to support our philosophy about respecting the property and feelings of others. I make sure to work into the discussion the fact that everyone has a right to come to school and to be safe and happy here. We also talk about manners and how students can make the classroom a more positive place to be.

I make a big deal of the contract. I get the principal to come in, and all the children sign in ink. He and I sign as witnesses at the bottom. I explain to children that, "This contract is to support our first goal of learning, and we will refer to it throughout the entire school year." I do refer to it a lot, especially in September. I try to be positive, to help children understand the benefits these rules have. For instance, rather than say, "We broke this rule today," I might say, "You know, I saw two children today who worked wonderfully well together. It is good to see how cooperation helps us all learn."

It's been my experience that kids who have discipline problems often don't understand what behavioral boundaries are; they're unfamiliar with the calming quality of limits. This contract is something concrete to help them learn the benefits of having limits. And by referring to it throughout the year, I go on helping them to understand its important implications.

DR. BRODKIN COMMENTS

Clear boundaries are a boon to children, provided, of course, that those boundaries are fair, consistent, and appropriate to children's developmental levels. Such parameters enable kids to feel protected, not only from others' potentially harmful behavior, but from their own. Remember, in childhood, the scariest impulses are usually those that might erupt from oneself. Even recalcitrant toddlers are reassured by the phrase, "I won't let you hurt someone." We adults need to provide and model safe limits for growing children until they have made them their own.

Universal boundaries are comforting, but, as always, we need to keep in mind individual needs for limit setting and for encouragement. It helps to allow children to see you as an individual person, too, rather than just "the teacher." These next few stories illustrate teachers' skills at balancing all of these, as well as other important considerations in making "the group" a sheltering place to grow.

RECOGNIZING INDIVIDUALS

On the first day of school I say, "Are you nervous, because I am." That breaks the ice right away. I also share my motto: I will always try to be fun, fair, firm, and consistent. I love teaching, and I believe that the kids like to be in my room. I like to be upbeat, energetic, fun, and fair—and I think that I am. I also tell children at the beginning of the year that I know that each one of them has special talents, special gifts, and special problems. One might be better at reading, one might be better at math, and another person might be a good speller or a great helper. There will be times when I deal with people differently. If they see me doing something for one person that I am not doing for another, they can question that; they can ask me about it. I might not always say why, but there will be a good reason, and it may have to do with the fact that everyone is different.

DR. BRODKIN COMMENTS

This teacher's openness to sharing her feelings works wonderfully well for her. Nothing goes further in establishing trust than the consistent demonstration of tuning in to the needs of each child, even if some temporary envy is the cost. I have always marveled at teachers' abilities to know and respond to individual differences in the classroom. It is difficult enough to accomplish this in families or even in one-on-one situations, but the payoff is wonderful for all when a child or adult feels understood. We're about to see how some teachers can achieve all this and still set forth clear expectations about cooperative behavior.

VERBALIZING EXPECTATIONS

In the beginning of the year I say to kids, "We are all going to be in the same room for 200 days, so we have to work together. I don't expect everyone to be best friends here. That wouldn't be natural. But I do expect everybody to be able to work together and to get along. Friendships are special, and you will make friends with whomever you choose." I share the fact that not all of the teachers at school are good friends but nevertheless, we work together. Then I let children know that I will be putting them in groups, and the groups will change throughout the year. I do a lot of group activities and mix kids with different personalities, so that they learn how to work with different people. I tell my students: "Sometimes in your group you will find—and this is a fact of life—that there will be someone difficult to work with. That is something you are going to have to learn to deal with. I'm not always going to be able to be there next to you, helping you work out problems. This is something I expect you to try and do."

These expectations may be a high reach for some children, but perhaps this teacher knew that this particular group could rise to the occasion. Some more beginning-of-the-year strategies follow.

STARTING WITH A CLEAN SLATE

In almost every school you hear stories about certain kids as they come up through the ranks: first grade, second grade. You hear rumors left over from years before and think, "Uh-oh, that kid's on my list." But I really try to take each kid from where he or she is when entering my room, and I don't care if last year's teacher had a terrible time with that particular child. I even tell the kids, "Teachers hear stories about some kids' past problems, but I don't listen. We have a clean slate together because I haven't gotten to know you yet. You can show me who you are, create your own up-to-date reputation based on what you do here." That pledge goes a long way.

I'll never forget the time one kid came up to me toward the end of the year and said, "That first day of school when you said you knew nothing about us, and you didn't know if we were troublemakers or not? Well, I had been a troublemaker and hearing that made me like you, so I decided I wasn't going to do that bad stuff to you."

FOUR SIMPLE RULES

We begin on day one establishing that everybody is important and unique, and that everyone has a different way of living his or her life. I talk about how we all come from a different place, and at the end of the day everyone goes home to a different place. But in our schoolroom, we can do important caring things for each other.

I emphasize four important facts: 1. We are in school to learn. 2. Everyone came in with smartness but each person's job is to grow even smarter. 3. This year, each person is going to grow in his or her appreciation of others and in how proud each of us is of ourselves. 4. I am a happy partner in making all that happen. In other words, I try to create the framework for a big picture with lots of examples, so children have positive behavior to emulate.

Then we develop class rules together, and I build in lots of time for us to recognize each other's positive behavior and qualities. For instance, I really like it when students notice what other people are doing for each other. When Manuel told me that he saw Maria invite Ashley to play in a game, I gave him verbal praise and then asked the class, "Who else heard something or saw something good happen?" We seek to recognize positive things rather than focus on and discuss what's not going right.

At the beginning of the year, I choose where children sit randomly. I put names on the tables and am careful to mix boys with girls. Then, as I learn who children are, I start adjusting the seating according to personality styles, making sure we don't have a table full of extremely strong people and another table of very quiet people. I want a social mixture and an academic mixture, so there are individualized opportunities for different children at each table. I also explain that I will continue to choose where everyone sits until May. Then they can write a note to tell me who they want to sit with and how good a job they are doing in school. (I don't let discussion take place aloud because that could be too painful.) In May I read everyone's notes and if I have a concern, the child and I discuss it. They know that, as they've learned from me throughout the year, not everything we want in life necessarily happens. This is their opportunity to put in requests, but I will make the final decision.

DR. BRODKIN COMMENTS

When you think about it, most, perhaps all, who succeed in establishing a calm classroom have this not-so-secret lucky charm of consistently "accentuating the positive and virtually eliminating the negative." At any rate, it is an invaluable goal to strive for.

Ten Hints for Setting Up and Keeping Your Classroom Conducive to Learning

As you strive to create an environment where children can learn and live together peacefully, take time to:

- Tune in to kids. Listen carefully, and empathize.

- Think about what children might be feeling and thinking. When students feel respected, they're more likely to respect others.

- Make your classroom a place where children feel safe, emotionally and physically.

- Reward, praise, and show your appreciation for appropriate behavior.

- Model the behaviors you're seeking.

- Trust your intuition when it comes to grouping children, and don't be afraid to change your mind.

- Demonstrate, over and over, that you believe in each child's ability to succeed.

- Keep in mind: The younger the children, the fewer the rules.

- Be positive and upbeat in your demeanor but also truthful about your own feelings.

- As you reflect on the strengths and challenges of each child and each class, adapt your expectations accordingly.

Keeping It Going All Year Long

In this section we discover teachers intuitively tuning in to individual needs. Their clear and positive expectations are so well timed and patiently applied that even most kids who begin the year out of sync eventually make the classroom ethic their own.

HELPING CHILDREN LEARN TO HANDLE CHOICES

In some ways, my classroom is not traditional at all. My students sit in groups because it's easier to communicate and to share and talk about ideas together. I have an independent writing time, which we call "Invitation Time," when the kids pick projects to work on, so my class is a little louder than a traditional classroom. However, sometimes I wonder if this environment doesn't encourage disruptive behavior, at least in some of the kids. Then I remind myself that years ago, when I did everything right from the workbook, I had huge discipline problems because it made school really boring, and everything we did was so predictable. When I changed the way I taught, when I gave my students opportunities to make choices—and there's so much power in choice— behavior problems began to diminish.

> **DR. BRODKIN COMMENTS**
>
> I agree. A great many seemingly emotional and social (i.e., behavior) problems arise at least in part as a protest against a feeling of powerlessness. On the other hand, a child who feels he or she has some influence on the learning and behavior expectations at school is much more likely to behave appropriately, out of pride of ownership.

I had this one little girl, Anna, who was very bright but was having such a hard time because she couldn't sit still. She was very verbal, very assertive with the other kids, pretty much of a leader, yet not always the kind of leader I wanted. In my classroom, her problems became issues of self-control.

I told her parents, "We're having a problem. I know Anna is smart and that she'll figure this out. We just have to help her and be patient together." I think for Anna, one of the most important parts of learning had to be knowing when and how to turn things on and turn things off. If I had put her in a more controlled environment she might have done what I told her, but in the long run she wouldn't have acquired the self-discipline she would really need for school and life. That's why I kept at it.

DR. BRODKIN COMMENTS

This is a very apt insight, and in my view, the teacher made a wise decision. Strict external control does not beget genuine self-control. We are fooling ourselves if we run a tight ship without some assurance that kids are learning and internalizing standards of appropriate and inappropriate behavior. The next two teachers share their strategies for helping kids internalize behavioral standards.

ENCOURAGING PERSONAL GROWTH

Starting in September we post a huge paper tree that is bare of any leaves. We call it our "Caring Tree." Anyone around the building who sees random acts of kindness fills out a little leaf certificate with the person's name and the act of kindness. And then once a month, at an assembly, we acknowledge these random acts of kindness and put the leaves on the tree. We talk about how our school goal is to totally fill the bare tree with leaves. We also have a black, empty sky which we hope to fill up with stars that stand for academic achievement and personal growth. I think both of these really help to build a sense of the school as a community. The criteria for acts of kindness and personal growth are broad enough to make sure that we don't end up recognizing only those kids who are always "nice."

ESTABLISHING A COMMUNITY OF SUPPORT

In September we establish the fact that all the children in the school belong to every teacher. That means that any teacher can call any student on his or her actions—in the hallways, on the playground, visiting another class, etc. Children learn that if anyone behaves inappropriately, that student may hear about it from a number of different sources, and so they begin to get the message. To us it translates to teachers supporting each other. It's not taking the positive road, but it is letting children know that there are consequences to their actions.

DR. BRODKIN COMMENTS

It may sound contradictory for me to agree with this policy. After all, I have urged the use of positive reinforcement. But I do feel this universal consistency of expectations has genuine value, as long as everyone involved is as likely to praise as to rebuke. Consistency plus genuine support nurtures children, as the next story illustrates.

PROVIDING THE RIGHT ATMOSPHERE

One year I had a child of average intelligence who chose not to speak. This particular girl, Kaitlin, came to me in my fourth-grade special education, communication-handicapped class. I didn't know anything about her. (I don't believe in reading anything about children before they come into my room, so I can give every child a fair chance.)

On the first day of school, I called roll and thought I heard Kaitlin say something, but I just went on to the next child. After I learned more about her, I remember telling her that I was happy she was in my room and that she could participate in any ways she wanted. She didn't ever have to feel that she had to answer; when she was ready, she would. In other words, I tried to do whatever I could to give her courage, to let her know that I was there for her, and that I wasn't going to force her in any way.

Looking back, I don't think there was a particular day when I thought, "Oh my God, she spoke." I think it just came gradually. I do remember someone in the teacher's room asking me how she was doing, and I said, "You know, I think she did say something today." Everyone was shocked. From kindergarten to third grade, most teachers had never heard her talk, although she did, at times, talk very quietly to a friend in a resource room where she went for an hour a day.

I wasn't the only reason for this success. Our classroom had a beautiful chemistry that worked for her. Maybe the experience of getting into a small and comfortable place, coupled with my very demonstrative (silly and gregarious) manner, was the key. Perhaps because she could laugh at me, she could see that if anyone was going to be made fun of, it would be the teacher, not her. Along the way I had to trust my instincts and feel in my gut what was right to do and when the rapport with the class would make this work. Most important, I knew that we needed to create an environment that was very, very safe.

There was no book to tell me how to deal with this particular child, so for a while I just watched. I noticed how she looked directly into children's eyes. I started to notice the times when she chose not to speak. One day, it seemed to me that something was bothering her. I remember that I noticed something in her body language. So, working on instinct, I asked her to turn her chair so that she didn't have to face us. Then I asked everyone to hold hands and give her good, positive energy. (The kids gave her a lot of positive encouragement.) And she spoke. In fact, she laughed, probably because she knew it was odd to speak to the wall. I don't know if this was the first time she spoke.

She always spoke quietly, but by the end of the year she was speaking. I was able to send her out to another classroom, to a teacher she liked, to ask for paper. Some years later, she came back from junior high to visit me, and she was talking, and that was just wonderfully gratifying. I felt that her turnaround had begun when we created a class environment that felt safe.

DR. BRODKIN COMMENTS

This compelling story demonstrates, among other things, the enormous value of thoughtful observation and empathy, as well as a teacher's willingness to make a leap of faith and base her decision on her own informed insight. Just as talented teachers can correctly judge a realistic reach for each child's academic growth, many also sense how and when to intervene behaviorally, and how and when to expect a reticent child to finally take risks. Notice how this next teacher uses her power of observation to carefully plan student seating in an effort to foster community-building and personal growth.

SEATING ARRANGEMENTS COUNT

Every nine weeks I change the seating in my room. I strategize where students should sit, pairing a kid who is very much a loner with somebody who's nurturing, helpful, and patient, so that child can encourage and help the other. I'll place a kid with a temper near someone who is calm and not as easily distracted. In fact, it takes me a couple of hours to figure out who should sit with whom, making sure tables are diverse in every way they can be. The kids don't know how carefully I plan this, though; they think I draw the names out of a hat. By the end of the year I've gone through countless combinations.

DR. BRODKIN COMMENTS

Flexible and creative seat planning can be very helpful. But we do have to look out for some hazards, such as labeling or stereotyping kids with certain traits. It's important to remain open to the possibility that children may move on and no longer fit those early labels. Another cautionary word: Under some circumstances, we may seem to be punishing the nice, quiet, calm, get-down-to-work kids by pairing them with those who have a penchant for getting into trouble. Being aware of these possible hazards should be enough.

Bringing Out the Best in Kids

In this section teachers share their experiences of enabling children to feel competent and appreciated, and to be considerate of others. The teachers have already learned that recognition and reward for any job well done are incentives to go on working hard. When the children are helped to recognize how important it is to be positive about others' accomplishments, in the words of one teacher, "The whole process is a real shot in the arm for everyone."

FOSTERING REFLECTIVE BEHAVIOR

In the beginning of school, almost every kindergartner blurts out whatever he or she wants to say. So we spend a lot of time talking about the importance of taking turns. For some kids it's easier than for others. All children need to feel that you're their advocate, and that you're asking them to do something for everybody's good, including their own. It is vital that they know you're not just being arbitrary or authoritarian ("This is what you must do because I say so").

I work hard to establish a respectful partnership with the kids so that everybody feels that what I'm asking is necessary for the good of our classroom community. When that idea gets through, kids start to help each other. A child's self-esteem doesn't suffer when he or she makes mistakes, because everybody is for everybody and has the same goals in mind.

I know that each child in my room is more cooperative because everyone knows I am not their enemy. I'm not trying to make children do things they can't do. Every time a child does something I'm trying to get him or her to learn to do, I reward his or her behavior. This can be just a word of praise, or a big smile, or walking over to the child afterward and saying, "Gosh, you did such a great job on the rug today." I try to make my comment one that helps children reflect on their behavior before acting, instead of being impulsive. This kind of interaction can help behavior improve quickly.

DR. BRODKIN COMMENTS

The first requisite for effective praise is that it be genuine. Kids are masters at detecting falseness. So you've got to mean what you're saying, be genuinely enthusiastic, yet not seem surprised that this child performed so well, for once again, your belief in the child's ability to do what he or she did is very important. Look for that little smile of gratitude for your appreciation, and be ready for even more of a "Can Do" attitude, which assures you that the deserved praise worked. This next teacher shares her more formalized reward system, which has some of the same potential benefits.

REWARD SYSTEMS CAN WORK

I have a big reward system, but it's not based on tangible rewards. Children earn class points, and after they've earned 100, they get to do something they want to do. That gives everyone power. For instance, my kids wear uniforms, and one day they wanted to have "free dress," so we decided that that would be a reward. Another day they wanted an hour of reading with pillows and teddy bears, so I made that a class reward they could work toward.

We also have table points or table compliments—helping your neighbor or the people at your table can earn a privilege such as popcorn on Friday. And we have daily rewards, which are small things like a little figurine of a gold Oscar that I found. All day long I observe the children and they observe each other. Then, at the end of the day, I say: "My Oscar winner is…" We do this over and over, and all they get is the same little Oscar figurine to put on their desk the next day, but they love it. (I'm convinced that the award could be anything—a two-thumbs-up sign, or a potted plant.) I also have everyone write down the name of someone they saw doing something great. They each acknowledge someone in the class and I do, too.

I've learned, though, that at the end of each day I have to make an effort to remember the specific thing (and this is the hard part for me) that a particular child did to earn the Oscar. I'll never forget the time a parent at a conference said to me, "My child has earned the Oscar only three times this whole year." And I thought, "Oh my gosh. I'm not even keeping track." Her child was wonderful and could succeed with her eyes closed for the rest of her life, but the comment made me realize that the kids I tended to favor were the ones who most needed the positive recognition. This girl's parent understood that; nevertheless, as she said, every kid deserves recognition. I promised the parent and myself that I would start keeping track to be sure that everyone gets an equal share.

> "We are an inner-city school, drawing on one of the lowest socio-economic groups around, and our kids have tough, poor home lives. What we try to say to every kid is: 'I understand that sometimes things are bad at home. I really can't change that. But you know that when you are here, this is a *different* place. When you walk through that door, you can make this place whatever you want it to be for yourself.'"
>
> —second-grade teacher

DR. BRODKIN COMMENTS

It's wonderful to be secure enough to accept a parent's constructive criticism. And there are so many potential positives from parent-teacher trust. We all have something to learn from one another, and when we can acknowledge that with ease, kids are the real winners. Read on for more teacher-designed methods of encouraging positive behavior.

CELEBRATING GOOD BEHAVIOR

We have a ticket system. If kids do something good or set a good example, I give them a ticket with a number on it. Every couple of weeks we have a raffle where I draw a number, and the person who has that number on his or her ticket gets to pick something out of the ticket basket. (Everything in the basket is just penny or dime stuff.) We also have a little ceremony where the person comes up and we all clap. No one is allowed to complain: "Oh why didn't I get picked?" I involve everyone in the excitement, and we clap and cheer and say, "Good for you!" We just make it a really big deal.

I think that even more than the excitement of having their number picked and choosing something out of the basket, children are just thrilled to be recognized and celebrated by their peers. It helps me, too. The whole ceremony gives me a chance to say to myself that we've done a good job this week, and it reminds me that I spend so much effort on being positive, because many of our children just don't get a lot of that in their lives.

LOOKING FOR GOOD BEHAVIOR

As part of my behavior system, I divide kids into groups. Children sit at five tables, and each table is a team. I list each team on the chalkboard. While kids are working I might ask them to stop briefly, so I can draw their attention to the fact that I'm going to give out points for working hard. I don't necessarily do it every time. I don't want them to be little behaviorist mice. But I do it sort of randomly—every once in a while—throughout the day. Before we go home, all the kids on the team with the most points get little stickers. (As many times as not, the whole class has the same number of points, so everyone is a winner.) Frankly, I really try to look for reasons to give points to everybody.

DR. BRODKIN COMMENTS

This teacher is another intuitive behavioral scientist. Research findings have shown that unpredictable intermittent rewards have a more lasting effect than predictable rewards. The kids in this classroom are more likely to internalize the teacher's expectations and feel good about themselves in future school situations. The next three stories demonstrate additional ways to use positive rewards for positive ends.

Teaming Up With a Colleague

Some reward systems work best in cooperation with another class. If, for example, there are end-of-the-week rewards for desirable behaviors, one teacher takes the kids who've earned the rewards, while the other teacher works with the kids who were less fortunate this time. Then, we switch the next week. Both "assignments" are important, since there is a special challenge in helping kids who hadn't succeeded become determined and optimistic about their chances for next time. No one comes away feeling like an inevitable failure.

Finding Individual Opportunities

One little boy I had wasn't getting his homework done, and he also wasn't getting the same support at home that most of my other students were getting. His name was Martin, and he lived with his dad, who kept saying he would help out, but he never did. I had a strong feeling that Martin wasn't participating or achieving as well as he probably could have. He just didn't pay attention, not even during shared reading or when I would use puppets with the kids (and I'm a pretty animated storyteller). I asked him to come in at lunchtime so I could find something special for him to do. (I'm usually in my room during lunch so I can give kids extra time.) Martin really loved the computer, so when he came in we would do that a little bit and also have a chance to talk.

We have a reading activity in my class where each kid gets a little race card that their parents are supposed to sign, saying they've read for 20 minutes or they were read to for 20 minutes. When they turn in their signed card, they get to roll the dice and move their own little guy along in a race. Anybody who finishes the race gets a certificate, and we have a party. I knew that an activity like this one could be a real setup for Martin, a daily dose of problems and negative experience. So I decided to use our lunchtime together to give him a chance to come in and read a little bit to me. I wouldn't make him do the whole 20 minutes, that would be taking too much time out of his recess. But at least he could be a part of the whole thing and not be left out. It really seemed to help and began to turn the tide for both of us.

Behavior Modification: Food for Thought

As soon as a child comes into my room, I try to find the very first positive thing he or she does and point it out in order to reinforce this positive behavior. However, it has been my experience that sometimes this well-meaning tactic can backfire, and I'm not sure why. I'm also not sure why one day you can have a great day with a child, and then the following day will be a really horrible one. Because I don't know what to do about either case, I've asked myself whether I should consider behavior modification techniques.

But I keep coming back to the fact that they seem like bribery to me and send a message to children that people are going to "pay" them every inch of the way when they do the socially acceptable thing. And if adults are willing to "pay" for desirable behavior, so to speak, why wouldn't a clever child withhold good behavior sometimes so he can continue to get paid for it?

DR. BRODKIN COMMENTS

If we limit our interaction with children—or adults, for that matter—to a rigid reward schedule, we sacrifice some of the richer benefits of communicating and relating. Many of the teachers' moving stories reported here point to the merits of meaningful interactions and the positive influence teachers can have when they tune in to kids' own thoughts and feelings. I suppose a strict behaviorist would say that these teachers were rewarding children with a sense of being understood and valued. Then, in that way, we are all behaviorists; yet, happily, most of us don't get bogged down in a mere mechanical technique, but try to focus mainly on children's individual needs and create an environment conducive to learning.

Talking and Listening to Children

IN THIS CHAPTER, teachers demonstrate the power of making children their partners. Sometimes there is a single teacher and child collaborating to master a behavioral challenge, while at other times, the whole class participates on behalf of the cause. Success requires understanding what matters to each person. No one style of intervention fits all, but the effort always involves respect for others and an awareness of individual needs. Being forthright about their own feelings and clear about the consequences of behavior often helps teachers to bring about a desired behavioral change. The following teachers' stories nicely demonstrate these points.

FINDING OUR WAY TOGETHER

I had a child in a fourth-grade class who was very bright and went from second grade straight to me, skipping third grade. Her parents were very pleased. A few years later they requested that their second daughter be placed in my room. Her name was Latisha. From experience, I knew the parents would be tough and question a lot, but I felt that was good for me. I soon learned that Latisha was not only gifted, but she was also withdrawn and socially inept—a triple challenge. Her older sister had been the model student, doing everything she should. Latisha tended to buck the system a little. She wouldn't do things she knew how to do. When I would ask her why, she'd say she didn't know.

I took a few months to observe and get to know her. Then I decided to try out a hunch. I have two signs hanging in my room: "Nobody can do everything, but everybody can do something," and "Always strive to do your very best." I took the second one and focused on it with Latisha. I told her that I was aware that she knew how to do a lot of the work. (From my observations, it had become clear that this was a kid who didn't need to do things over and over. If she could do something right the first time, she understood the underlying lesson.) I began to tailor what I asked her to do. For instance, I wouldn't ask her to do the same kind of math problems for five days. Instead, I told her that if she understood the lesson she would only need to do it for one day, and then I would use her as a peer tutor. She loved that. That was her thing. So Monday or Tuesday we'd give each other a look of "Do you get it?" "Yes." "Then let me give you a test, because I'm not looking to waste time making you do this." When she tested out of the homework, some of the kids might say, "How come Latisha doesn't have to do this?" And I'd say (referring to the other sign), "Here's one of those situations we've talked about. All of us are good at one thing, and Latisha is very, very good academically. But (I'd say lightheartedly), just like me, she's not so good artistically."

However, I also came to understand that she wasn't happy at home, and that school, no matter how forlorn she might look there, was really the high point of her day. So I made sure that when she was in school, it was good for her. I can remember one time when I sat her down and said, "Latisha, you know you're not doing what you need to be doing for me. And together, we need to somehow make this work, because you're going to be here for seven hours a day." Then I asked her what she didn't like about school, and she told me that she was bored.

At that point I decided to use a contract with her and said, "Okay, give me some ideas of what you would like to do." She started talking about marmots, and I asked her what a marmot was. (I wasn't sure and neither were the other kids.) I asked her to do a report and present it to the class. This was the kind of thing she ate right up. I also found that it worked if I put her in a group of three or four kids working on something she did well and they didn't. I also found that if there was something she didn't do so well, I could put her in a group with a few kids and a helper. Then, being very careful not to embarrass her, I pointed that out to the class. I wanted them to know that just because she often taught a group, that didn't mean that sometimes she couldn't learn from someone else.

As we made our way through the year together, the class seemed to grow in understanding others' varying capabilities, and Latisha had found a place where she could learn, even excel, and what is more, feel comfortable much of the time.

DR. BRODKIN COMMENTS

This last story and the one that follows illustrate the power of a classroom community united in the effort to help one member.

MAKING IT A GROUP EFFORT

I had a student, Victor, who was having real problems relating to other kids on the playground. No matter what activity we were engaged in, he had an incredibly hard time. I didn't want to embarrass him by tackling his problem with the entire class. I didn't think he could handle that emotionally. So, on a day when he was absent, I decided to involve the other kids (in as positive a way as possible) and talk about the difficult time Victor was having by asking them: "What can we do to help?" The kids came up with some ideas and sort of teamed up to play with him, pull him into some games, and just try to completely accept him. Of course, it wasn't always easy. There were times when the children would come to me and say, "You know, we're really trying, but he does this, this, and this." At those times, we'd come together and deal with whatever the issue was. I might say: "Victor, you were involved in this game and this happened. Can you tell us why?" Yes, there were frustrating times, but we had a real group effort. He knew it, I knew it, and the class knew it, and that made a great deal of difference.

DR. BRODKIN COMMENTS

Note how these teachers knew when to call for a group effort and when to focus directly on an individual child's needs.

TALKING TO CHILDREN ABOUT THEIR BEHAVIOR

I deal with children on a kid-by-kid basis. That means that in different years I might deal differently with kids who exhibit similar behaviors, because there are significant differences in what the kids' needs are. Hopefully, by the time there is a problem, I will have gotten to know who each kid is, so my first effort is to find the hook that is going to mean something to each student. For instance, if a child has really disruptive behavior, the first couple of times I'll usually just talk to her, heart to heart, just the two of us, and let her know how I see her behavior, how I feel it's affecting her, not only as a learner but as a person, and how it might affect other people relating to her as well.

I try to go about this by appealing to children's hearts. Sometimes they really respond and we become partners. I might say, "Okay, how can we make it so that you can keep yourself together? What strategies can we use?" I remember working with one boy who was fairly explosive once in a while. Together, we decided that he could give me a signal and then simply leave the room to pull himself together. He didn't abuse the privilege, because we had set up the parameters. It worked for him, and it worked for me. As time went on, I was able to help him recognize when trouble was about to happen. Then he began to pick up the warning signs of his imminent loss of control in time to prevent it.

Over the years, I have found that no matter how young kids are, you can talk with them honestly about their behavior and about its effect on how

> 66 I think it's extremely important not to react with yelling or to ever verbally belittle a child. We also mustn't belittle what parents are doing, because what they are doing may be all they know how to do. And we mustn't think that we, alone, have the complete right answer for every child. Most of us, even as adults, are still working on who we are. How can we have the perfect answer for each member of a class of 28 children? 99
>
> —third-grade teacher

other kids feel about them. Most can deal with that, and they are grateful, since everyone wants to be liked. They begin to see that if angry feelings start snowballing within them, the bad old patterns get called up, and they behave without thinking or without realizing the social consequences. When I see these problematic patterns, I tell the child that I know he's a really wonderful person, but my concern is that others will begin to see him as somebody who causes problems, and that is going to affect his relationships. I know even second graders can get this. After all, what you're saying is: "You do this and this is what happens. Are you comfortable with that? Is that what you want?"

DR. BRODKIN COMMENTS

This teacher holds a mirror up to the child and invites him to make an informed choice about the consequences of his behavior. In doing so, the teacher is giving the child a precious gift—a new opportunity for free choice, through insight and reason. It's the promise of freedom from the grip of mindless impulse. The next teacher uses a similar strategy with equal success.

DON'T BE AFRAID TO INDIVIDUALIZE

I had a student who was on medication for behavior problems, but he still had peaks and valleys, and at times, for one reason or another, he didn't take the full dosage. It was rough on our entire class. However, over time I realized that it was very important to him to remain in the classroom, so I used this knowledge as a hook. If he was becoming a problem, I would simply come up to him and whisper in his ear, "Brian, if this continues you're going to have to go outside, take five or ten minutes, and pull it together." He would agree to that because he wanted so badly to be involved in the class.

Now this was a kid who got out of his seat, distracted other kids, talked incessantly, rifled through his backpack, all things that could just drive the other kids crazy. They didn't want to sit by him, and they couldn't work near him. But we did work out a system, and as the year went on, he really progressed. When he began to be disruptive, I could put my hand on his shoulder as a silent signal, as if to say: "I recognize what you're doing and it's not okay." He grew to be able to use this as a cue to pull himself together.

DR. BRODKIN COMMENTS

But such success is not inevitable. The story below shows us that a teacher's genuine concern and great zeal sometimes are just not enough to overcome powerful barriers.

LEARNING FROM TOUGH SITUATIONS

I had a student a few years ago who, the minute he walked in the door on the first day of school, I characterized as someone I needed to focus on. In fact, I turned myself inside out. I did everything I knew how to do. He was angry. He was intelligent. He was creative, and he didn't do the work. He had a temper, and he did what he wanted to do. I tried to find out what he was interested in. I had heart-to-heart talks with him. I genuinely loved this kid, and I really wanted him to succeed. I got him into friendship groups. He actually ended up, socially, in a great group; there couldn't have been a better one for him. But at the end of the year, I didn't see much progress, and this was a kid whom I had really wanted to turn around.

What kept me going? I sensed and saw at times that he had a remarkable heart inside of him. He was the kid you wanted to take home and love until he blossomed. Unfortunately, he had a real young mom. She was still growing up herself and not sure of what to do with her son, so he was on his own a lot. His behavior became so bad that the principal actually said to him, "Why don't we send you home for the last two weeks of school." But the kid was adamant, and said, "No, I want to be here. I want to be here."

I do remember that at some point, I felt I had to be totally honest with him, so I said, "You are so intelligent and so creative, you have so many incredible ideas, and yet I see you on track to becoming a dropout." He looked at me and said, "No. I'm not going to drop out." So I said "Alberto, you've already dropped out. You're here in body but…" And I could see, for just a moment, a glimmer of understanding in his eyes. Then he just shut down again. Another time I told him, "I see all these people really caring about you. I care about you. Counselors care about you. And the kids care about you. The only person who seems not to care about you is *you*. People can only give to you for so long. When they see that you don't care, and you're not willing to make the effort to meet them even a quarter of the way, they're going to start giving up on you. That really scares me, because you are such a neat kid."

So I sent him on to the next grade, feeling strongly that I had lost him. And by seventh grade, they had him on half days, and then I think he ended up in community school. It just broke my heart. I tried everything I knew how to do.

It's just so hard sometimes, because those kids with problems stand out and capture your attention and your energy. And we forget to pause and realize that there may be 26 other kids we're touching, moving along, and making an impact on. That's what can be so frustrating: trying to balance, trying to remember that you have these other kids who need you just as much. It's incredibly tough stuff, and I don't even begin to think that I know the answers. I teach. I discipline. I read stuff and take things in, and go to workshops. But when it comes right down to it, it's "just a hunch from my gut" as to what this particular kid needs to hear in order to recognize what's happening and to cope a little better.

DR. BRODKIN COMMENTS

This is a remarkable revelation. It helps us to see that there is much private joy, as well as much private pain, in "teaching from the gut." Doing so demands great courage, and it takes strength to acknowledge that everything you can do may not be enough for one child, while less than everything you can do is more than enough for others. I hope this teacher appreciates her gift for blending knowledge, experience, devotion, and a great well of empathy in her dealings with children. Sometimes, as in the next example, a teacher sharing his or her frank insights can work wonders.

TELL IT LIKE IT IS

I've found it's important to demystify whatever you think is wrong with a child's behavior by helping the youngster to understand what you want him or her to do. For instance, I might say, "Brianna, when we have group conversations, I want you to contribute, because you have so much to say." Or, "When it comes to writing, this is the part that you have trouble with, so why don't you dictate to me or to someone else." Over the years, I've come to realize that I sometimes assume a child can intuit what I see as the problem, and that may not be the case. However, I've learned that things truly get better when I can put what I'm feeling and seeing into words. Children, then, have been able to understand and use the knowledge that I offer them nonjudgmentally. In fact, sharing my view often works wonders.

DR. BRODKIN COMMENTS

And like the teacher who comments next, if you can keep the child's life situation in mind, you are more likely to earn his trust.

CONSIDER CHILDREN'S REALITY

It's so important to be aware of, and to not deny, when something is wrong in a child's life or when something is painful. The mother of one of my children had cancer. As her cancer got worse, so did his behavior. One day he came in and said his neck was stiff. (I knew this was because she had bone cancer, and her neck was stiff.) I chose to deal with this very respectfully, accepting the problem just as it was reported: "I'm sorry. Try to do what you can today and let me know if your neck is better or worse later." I had to acknowledge the child's pain as he presented it to me.

DR. BRODKIN COMMENTS

It is imperative that we acknowledge when something is very wrong in a child's life, even though it may be painful. This teacher knows how important it is to see the world from the child's perspective. Doing that entails knowing facts as well as sensing feelings. She knows too that sometimes it is better to accept a child's version of reality than to risk undermining his tenuous stability. The importance of respecting a child's feelings is reaffirmed by the following vignette.

TAKING THE DIRECT APPROACH

I try never to single out a child in front of the class and say, "What's your problem?" If a child is just having a bad day, I take her aside at recess and talk to her, or we go in the back of the room and I'll say, "What can we do to fix this situation? Is something wrong? Is something bothering you today? Because I know you don't act like this always."

This approach gives children the chance to save themselves, in a way that does not embarrass them or put them down. I might say, "Something must be wrong today because you're not able to follow the directions. Could you tell me? Did you have breakfast?" "Did you have a fight with someone?" "Did something happen in your family?" Usually I can help them feel safe enough to tell me what's wrong, if they can identify it. Then I can enlist their help by saying, "How can I help you be successful today?"

DR. BRODKIN COMMENTS

Few children could resist the lure of such a respectful invitation to succeed. Once again the crucial lesson is: Consideration and respect can often turn a child around, while rebuke and punishment are more likely to do the opposite.

▶

> **W**e see so many kids who are dealing with things at home that we don't have the power to change, and yet we have to deal with the fallout at school. It's tough for us, but it's also so tough for them. Knowing what they have to deal with, sometimes I wonder how they can actually make it through the day and stay as sane as they are.
>
> —second-grade teacher

But what about the common situation of a child not being able to describe what is bothering him or her? Should we still probe and delve for an answer to the question, "What is wrong?" My suggestion is not to press the matter. After all, we adults often don't know what has incited our own occasionally poor moods, so why should we expect it to be easy for children to do this at all times? What's more, not being able to come up with an answer might make a child feel even more like a failure, and an answer given under duress may not tell the real or whole story anyway. Despite the lessons of pop psychology about the urgency of insight, it isn't always wise to strip individuals of defenses against knowing their own innermost thoughts. For example, a given child might be better off feeling relatively safe in the classroom by forgetting the troubles he faces elsewhere. Then the challenge is to make the classroom as much of an oasis as possible. Having clear rules and expectations, positive consequences for meeting them, and empathy for struggles to do so often can go a long way toward calming even the child who lacks insight about the source of his disquiet. And, as the next few stories show us, if we are honest about the way our own feelings influence our behavior, we can provide a valuable model for children.

BEING HONEST

We teachers talk and think about whether we are bringing our own problems to our work. I think that's a very important question. As for me, I went through four years of tough medical issues, and I actually think teaching was my salvation. School was a safe place for me. I didn't have to think about what was going on in my own life because I was too busy with the kids. They actually helped me more than they ever could have known. I don't think I've ever taken anything out on them, but there have been days when I'm short, so I always tell them, "I'm really having a bad day today. I need you to help me so that we all don't have bad days. I need you to cooperate with me, and if I ask you to do something, I would like you to do it the first time." Or if I was sick I would say, "I really don't feel well. Anything you can do to make it a better day for me will make it a better day for you." Fifth graders understand, and they completely respect the honesty. They get it because they know what it's like to have a bad day. Now sometimes when they're having a bad day, they tell me, "I'm having a really bad day today." And I can say, "Yeah, it stinks, doesn't it? But it's okay. You're not always going to get an 'A' on a test; you're not always going to be able to behave your best. We'll work through today together."

SPEAK FRANKLY

I had a group of girls who were sometimes in a "best-friend mode" with each other, while other times they seemed to just hate each other. During their off days, the girls had no trouble talking about each other, which caused many tears, trips to the bathroom during lessons, and various other disruptions. Sometimes it helped to talk to them. For instance, when Sasha felt left out because the rest of the group wouldn't sit with her at lunch, I decided to intervene. I got the other girls together and said, "If I went to the lunchroom, and there was a new teacher sitting all by herself at an empty table, and there was also a table full of my friends and an empty seat, where do you think I should sit?" And they said, "Oh, you should probably go sit with the new teacher who's all by herself." "I agree. Does this situation sound familiar?"

I'm not a big lecturer, but I do try to put things in terms children can understand and relate to. Then I follow up by speaking more directly. "We need to agree on something right now. I know you're angry with Sasha, and I can't change that. But what I can change is any possibility that your anger is going to affect my classroom. You're not going to run to the bathroom in tears, and you're not going to disrupt lessons. The problem you're dealing with is obviously too big for me to handle, so you're going to have to handle it on your own. Please do that, and please try not to hurt people's feelings. And for now, let's agree that this is not going to get in the way of our learning." It worked.

DR. BRODKIN COMMENTS

Sometimes, as in the following example, it is best to shift responsibility to the children themselves.

HELPING CHILDREN SEE AND MAKE CHOICES

Giving children choices—that's probably my number-one strategy. Shifting the task of finding a solution from the teacher to the kid: "I know you want to be a part of this, but if you start hitting or getting silly, you're going to have a choice to make, because you're not going to be able to stay in the room. You can go down the hall, we can call your mom to come and get you, or you can behave appropriately. The choice is yours." If a child says, "I don't want to do that," I say, "Well, you always have an option; you can do this instead." Of course, the "instead" is not something very exciting, but at least they feel that they don't just have to do something because the teacher says so. They take responsibility for their actions and know the consequences of their choices. They have to think and make a decision.

I also try to give children opportunities to think about and change *the way* they want to act. I've sent a child away from a particularly exciting project because he chose to behave a certain way. Then ten minutes later he came back and said, "Can I come in now?" So I said, "Let's talk about it. What do you need to do to be a part of the group?" And he said, "Stop hitting people and calm down." "Great! I agree." He made it for about three hours before he had to go out again.

DR. BRODKIN COMMENTS

There are so many potential benefits from reframing *limit-setting* as *having choices*. As the teacher pointed out, it provides the child with the sense of being the decision maker. It also brings the capacity for reason into its rightful place in a developing child's life. It puts in bold relief concern about consequences of behavior. And making choices allows for the growth of a sense of mastery. Still, a particular child may find mastery illusive, as we see in the next example.

WORKING WITH CHRONIC ANGER

I had one child, Taylor, who would often act out in anger. I knew that he had at least witnessed physical violence at home. One day he was playing with the dollhouse and bashing things all around. So I said to him, "That's so rough. I wonder why." And then I'd watch, and he'd go to another toy and he'd be rough again, and I'd say, "You seem upset today. I'd like to help. Can you think of something relaxing that we could do together? How about reading a story?"

DR. BRODKIN COMMENTS

Unfortunately, there are children who bring great personal burdens to school. The realities of a child's life may be so overwhelming that the only way a teacher can help is to demonstrate the desire to help. Offering to read a story or do something else together that the child might enjoy is a gift of kindness. It won't solve all the problems, but it may begin to make school a refuge. In the next story, a teacher shows how she comes to understand what it would take to successfully guide a particular child toward behavioral change.

INDIVIDUALIZING STRATEGIES TO MEET TOUGH CHALLENGES

I had one child who, from the beginning of the year, would just call out whenever he wanted to. When I thought about it, I realized his behavior was getting my attention. It wasn't positive attention, because I was constantly telling him not to do that. Nonetheless, it was attention. That made me realize that I had let myself be caught up in his game, so I decided to change my ways. When he started calling out, I wouldn't say anything to him. I would just hold up my hand, nod, turn to someone else and say, "Thank you so-and-so for putting up your hand and waiting for me to call on you." I did this consistently for a good week or two, and he finally started picking up on it. Then, as soon as I could, I started giving him positive feedback: "You know what? Today you didn't call out even one time! That was really good. I'm so glad you put your hand up. You were involved in everything, but you weren't calling out." He helped me learn that a key in working with children is looking for positive behavior and not getting caught in connecting with a child only by saying "no, no, no, no."

This same child had a tough family situation, going back and forth between his mom and his stepmom, who didn't get along, so sometimes it was hard for him to focus on daily activities. Instead, he would try to get another child off task. So I would call him up and say, "You know what? You cannot handle this right now. I want us to take a few minutes out to help you settle down." I didn't make him leave the room or have a time-out, which would be too obvious. I'd just say, "Why don't you get a book and go to the reading area, and then you can come back when you think you're ready." And when he came back, I'd ask him if he was ready to handle what we were doing, which gave him the opportunity to reflect. Monday mornings were particularly tough, and sometimes he'd come in and be really loud. When that would happen I'd just say, "Excuse me. You're back at school now. You know what's expected of you here. It is different from home. You need to start the day all over, and let's make it more positive." And I'd ask him to leave and re-enter, and as he did I'd remark, "O.K. The negative stuff is finished, let's start over again positively."

DR. BRODKIN COMMENTS

No two children pose exactly the same challenge in the same way. The next story presents a different teacher with a puzzle that he does manage to solve.

WORKING WITH A CHILD WHO TATTLES

I had one young boy who carried tattling to an extreme. His name was Danny. His parents didn't show up for parent conferences, so I had to deal with it on my own. In our school we have children from all over the world—Vietnam, Croatia, Iraq, Liberia. Danny's family had recently come to this country. He was the youngest of five children, with two older brothers. I wasn't sure if there was some cultural explanation for his behavior that I didn't understand. Perhaps when he tattled at home, his older brothers got punished for their misdeeds, so Danny ended up getting some mileage out of it.

Starting in the beginning of the year, Danny would come to me saying, "So-and-so's doing this," or "So-and-so's not doing his work." He might report something that happened on the playground or who was getting in an argument. I really didn't want this to become a pattern, so I would say, "Were you involved?" "No." "Then," I'd ask, "why are you telling me this?" That usually gave him pause, and I could follow by saying, "I know you're concerned, but if two other kids are having a disagreement, they know they can come to me with their problem. Unless you can give me a reason why you need to be involved…" So every time he would tattle I would restate this. There were still times when he would come up to me during class with reports that so-and-so wasn't working. And I would again say to him, "If it is something personally affecting you or involving you, then tell me. But, if it isn't, then it's my job to watch over everybody. I will deal with everybody else individually. You wouldn't want others to be involved when I am dealing with you, would you?" I think because I've been so consistent since September, the tattling has quieted down.

DR. BRODKIN COMMENTS

There is probably no single explanation for tattling. One child may have concluded that it is the most reliable way to acquire adult recognition, particularly if he does not feel optimistic about succeeding academically or socially. Another child may feel ignored and lost in the crowd unless he stirs up trouble. Some who are the youngest in the family have discovered tattling as the most reliable weapon in a rivalrous situation. In any case, as this teacher understood, consistently ignoring or devaluing the tattling helps to diminish it. Enabling such a child to enjoy an earned sense of mastery may eventually eliminate the urge to tattle. Teachers can rightfully ask for a new beginning with a more satisfactory ending, as the next example shows.

TAKE A BREATHER

If a child and I have had a rough week due to his or her behavior, at the end of that week I'll acknowledge it and say something like: "You know what? We had a rough week. Come Monday, we need to start over." Often kids will respond to this approach. It's a good feeling to know that you can start fresh. And it also gives me time over a weekend to think: "Okay, what can I do differently?"

DR. BRODKIN COMMENTS

But no one is effective all the time.

BE REAL

Of course there are days when things don't go well. I remember one time when I was supposed to read to the children, but they were acting just terribly. So I said: "You know what? Reading a book to you is one of my most pleasurable experiences. But right now, I'm really fed up with you guys, and I am not going to pretend to enjoy your company. I just feel too angry and upset, so I've set out some independent work for you to do, and I am going to my desk to work. We're going to be away from each other until I can calm down." After about half an hour I said, "Okay, now I'm over it. We can go back and carry on the day." To me, among other things, that's useful modeling. It demonstrates to children that I can be upset, I can remove myself from the situation, work it through, and then carry on.

DR. BRODKIN COMMENTS

This is a lovely vignette that demonstrates another way to encourage empathy. After all, everyone has feelings that can be hurt, including teachers. Perhaps even more valuable is the subtle modeling this teacher offers—and we can't overemphasize the power of modeling. Keep in mind that "Do as I say, not as I do" is not a wise motto for adults who want to set a positive and effective tone for acceptable behavior. And empathy can be enhanced, as we see in the following description.

Building Empathy

We may learn some day that a significant portion of the capacity for empathy has genetic origins. However, that does not mean it will be set in genetic stone; in fact, empathy requires environmental opportunity. As you work with children, keep in mind that early experiences can contribute to—or take away from—the development of empathy. Consider the following:

🌸 Children who have felt understood as infants, toddlers, and youngsters are most likely to become empathic individuals. There are exceptions, of course. A minority of highly empathic people may have missed out on empathic care but compensate later in life by tuning in to others' needs.

🌸 Empathic adults are positive influences. It is invaluable for children to witness empathic behavior. A caring classroom, with examples set by all of the adults present, can be a powerful contributor.

🌸 Positive early experiences that build trust and attachment and foster optimism allow children the freedom to develop empathy.

🌸 Self-centeredness and selfishness in children's environments may inhibit the growth of empathy. Being around adults who are preoccupied, depressed, or short-sighted about the world outside themselves does not build empathy.

🌸 Living among very real dangers, such as threats to life or serious illnesses, can make the development of empathy an unaffordable luxury. A sense of safety is definitely a prerequisite.

🌸 When you (and other adults who are important in children's lives) underscore and praise the behavior of children who show concern about other people's feelings, you foster the development of empathy.

There continues to be controversy in the field about when empathy may begin to develop. Some consider the crying of an infant or toddler in response to the crying of another child to be an early sign of empathy. Certain toddlers and many preschoolers try to comfort a peer who is obviously upset, sometimes by volunteering the aid of their own mothers. Are these the signs of early empathy? Or does true empathy require the maturity to suspend one's own identity, however briefly, in order to have a true sense of what it must be like to be the other person? The jury is still out on the semantics. But, by school age, most children are open to a positive influence.

TAKING ANOTHER PERSPECTIVE

If a child says something mean to someone else, I ask, "How would you feel if I said…?" and I pick something particular to that child. For instance, if the child's not a very good speller, I'll say, "You know, Jonathon, you're not as good at spelling as you are at some other things. How would you feel if so-and-so said, 'You stink at spelling.'? That would hurt your feelings, wouldn't it?" In other words, I try to put children in a particular person's place so we can talk about it.

In this chapter, we have heard and seen teachers tuning in to children who have problematic behavior. The children's needs, feelings, and interests, even their ambivalence about changing or exercising greater self-control, have been thoughtfully considered. Often children are faced with the dilemma of wanting to be liked and accepted without considering the effect their behavior has had on others. When appropriate, the group's support was sought on behalf of the struggling child. And, also when appropriate, the children were frankly, but respectfully, confronted with choices they must make and the potential outcomes of those choices. The many successes reported seem to result from an honest collaboration of teacher and child.

Working with Parents

PROBLEMATIC BEHAVIOR IS MOST LIKELY TO BE OVERCOME
by a team effort of the teacher, parent, and child. Children whose
teachers and parents develop a mutually trusting and respectful relationship
have a definite advantage. For many reasons, however, parents often are not
available to work with teachers. Some are just too busy keeping their own heads
above water; others are apprehensive or uncomfortable in a school setting. The
teachers we interviewed recognized the importance of enlisting parents'
involvement whenever possible. Some did what they could to be supportive of
parents, and that helped. Other teachers discovered that they had no option but
to do what they could without the parents' support. The stories included here
provide strategies teachers have found effective for enlisting parent support.

WORKING TOGETHER FOR A POSITIVE CONSEQUENCE

Parents' involvement is vital for making constructive behavioral change.
When there's a problem, I ask the parents to come in with their child and sit
down with me. I talk about exactly what I'm seeing, and then involve the
student by asking him or her, "How are we going to set it up so this behavior
doesn't continue? It's not okay for you, it's not okay for the rest of the kids in
the class, and it's not okay for me." We work out a plan together. Often a
weekly report goes home to the parents who have already worked out a
reward system, such as planning to go to a movie together if the child
improves during the week. It's all based on working together for a positive
consequence, rather than telling the child he's going to lose something,

because the latter doesn't seem to work very well. If I see that the plan isn't working, I give the parents a call and say, "You know, we've been trying, but I don't really see much of a change, so we need to go to something a little bit tighter, a little bit more strict."

DR. BRODKIN COMMENTS

Some might question whether the answer to this parent-teacher dilemma is to get stricter with the child. Perhaps, a more sensitive approach would be to put their heads together again and try to understand why the child is resistant to changing his behavior, and how the adults may better motivate him. This means pooling their knowledge about what does matter to him. In the comment that follows, another teacher explains how important it is to get the parents' input; but what a challenge that can be if a teacher has limited opportunities to assure the parent that his or her perspective is truly valued by the school.

WORKING TOWARD PARENT INVOLVEMENT: ONE-ON-ONE

I feel quite strongly that parents need to know how important their involvement in school is to their kids. I remember, early in my career, having a night where I encouraged all the parents to come in. It was really a flop. Hardly anybody came. But I did get the feeling that a lot of the kids had trouble with school because the parents probably also had had troubles when they were in school, so school was not a place that they thought of as safe and warm. I knew I needed to find ways to alter that idea. I found that sometimes it would help if I asked parents to come in about a specific problem (because they just stayed away as long as they thought that everything was going okay). Then I tried to find something that would help us relate on a personal level. For instance, I knew Eugene's father was a construction worker, and I had worked a little at construction with my father-in-law during the summers. When he came in to talk about a problem his son was having, I related stories to him about my experiences in the construction business, and that seemed to break the ice. Then I went over the days Eugene would almost always have homework—Tuesdays and Thursdays—so that he would know when to look for it. At the same time, I tried to emphasize some positive points and followed up by saying that I thought it was very important that Eugene see the two of us talking, so he would know that school wasn't something that he would have to deal with alone. We were able to set a time up a month later when we would talk again, and we did. Plus, I was able to say to Eugene soon after, "I talked to your dad, and he seemed very interested in your doing a little better." The boy was very interested in the fact that his dad had come to school. Now I had something I could build on.

> **I**'m sticking with the thought that young children are still very much tied in to their families. Their history in the world is so short that their home life is the real fertile ground from which they have come. Because each child is shared between home and school, I think we in education have a lot to gain by tapping into that home knowledge.
>
> —kindergarten teacher

> *More often than not, if you expect good things from children, you get them. I have high expectations for my kids, and the parents support me.*
>
> —fourth-grade teacher

DR. BRODKIN COMMENTS

The next teacher offers us a sample of her approach to parent conferences.

BUILDING A TEAM

When a child is having a problem, I invite the parents in for a conference and say, "This is what I'm seeing that particularly concerns me. Can you help? What do you think it is all about?" If they choose to say, "I have no idea," that's when I say, "Well, we've got to find out. You don't know what to do, and I don't know what to do, and I'm really concerned for your child. His behavior is getting in the way of his learning."

I can remember a few times when a parent said she had noticed the behavior and checked with her pediatrician, who said it was normal. In those cases I've learned to reply, "Gee, I'm surprised to hear that the pediatrician said that, because I've dealt with children for many years, and I find this unusual. Maybe we ought to have some other professionals help us out." Then I describe what our child-study team is like and how they can help. I also say, "I'd like to introduce you to the principal so you can also discuss this with him." If a parent asks my opinion on private counseling, I am positive and may also offer a list of recommended people. And I always let the parents know that I'm more than willing to speak with any professional with whom they're working.

DR. BRODKIN COMMENTS

Many teachers are uncomfortable about making referrals, either within the school community of experts or privately. It may be helpful to frame the recommendation in the following way: "You know, you and your child are entitled to have the benefit of our experts' opinions." You might even go so far as to say, "Your tax money pays for this opportunity; why not take advantage of it?" Also, put yourself squarely on the parent's side: "Let's not look upon this as anyone's failure—either yours or mine—but rather as something that happens in the course of growing up. Still, if you would be more comfortable going outside of the school community, I'll certainly understand. I myself will welcome the opportunity to have expert guidance about helping your child, either from someone here, in an outside community agency, or in a private setting. Just let me know what I can do." In the next vignette, a teacher shares her method of making parents feel welcome and respected.

KEEPING COMMUNICATION OPEN

At our school, parents have a set time for visitation, but I try to encourage them to come in whenever they can. I send home a newsletter, once a month, telling parents what's going on. I also try to keep them very active, which I think is key. I let them know: "I need a volunteer to help with a science experiment. I need a volunteer to do…" I'll put "Help Needed" or "Help Wanted" ads in the newsletter and list what I need, and some of the parents apply. It's really cute, and it works.

I don't hesitate to call a parent at any time for something bad, but I also don't hesitate to call for something good. It surprises parents, but they love just hearing that their kid had all his homework done or worked really hard that day.

DR. BRODKIN COMMENTS

There is no greater gift to a parent than unexpected positive news. That is reason enough to follow this teacher's lead. In addition, doing so builds parent-teacher trust that may be invaluable in some future situation. Building on the combined understanding of teachers and parents can sometimes result in valuable discoveries for both, as we see in the next story.

SUPPORTING CHILDREN AND THEIR PARENTS

I had a child who was willing to participate but initiated very little. She did some eye avoidance—a lot of downcast looking. At other times she would watch very intently, but would not give away anything on her face that might be read as a reaction. The other children thought of her as very quiet. She'd sit with them, but not offer very much. Her name was Grace. Over time, watching and being with her, I started to rule out any emotional issues and began to feel that she might not be hearing everything that was going on. Her parents were very caring, and her mom had told me that Grace had always been quiet, so they thought that this was just her way. I shared what I thought, and recommended that they take her to have her hearing tested. They did, and found out that she had a significant hearing loss that was having a major effect on her behavior.

Grace got a hearing aid for each ear and became a reader and a writer. She spoke more with children, and there was a brightness in her eyes that had not been there before. She had only been able to interact with the world as she knew it. Now she had the opportunity to discover so much more.

Of course, her parents felt just terrible that they had missed this for so long. I addressed their feelings by explaining to them that there will always be things that we don't know, that I am a mother of two children, and there are some things I never would have missed in a perfect world. I worked hard to stroke

> ## "Sometimes a child's problem may not be social or emotional. As watchers of children, we have to be open to a myriad of other possible explanations."
>
> —fifth-grade teacher

and embrace these parents, because they had been open to hearing the message to get help. They had always felt that they had a bright child, but that she didn't seem to show her brightness in easily measured ways. She hadn't been experiencing the fullness of the world around her. In the end, they didn't have trouble coming to grips with their child's hearing impairment. In fact, they were actually grateful that it was a situation they could do something about.

DR. BRODKIN COMMENTS

But of course, not every parent and teacher can be trusting collaborators. Here is one example.

GETTING REAL

I have learned that if I speak to a parent and the parent doesn't choose to share information, or if that parent resists my observations and insists on her own point of view, I have to accept this as reality for the time being. When we're getting nowhere, therefore, I close the conversation by saying, "I've heard what you shared with me," and I restate the parent's remarks. She may have denied that her child has done something inappropriate, or redefined the situation, putting her child in a more favorable light. If that is what becomes clear, I have to be aware that this is how the parent chooses to live. I have to say that she has made her decision, which I respect, but the fact is that if her child's behavior does not conform to the rules of school, we will have to address that situation here, as we see fit, without her help.

Six Quick Tips
for Working with Parents

- Start out positive, and stay that way as long as you can.
- Admire children's good qualities.
- Ask for parents' support while demonstrating you are on their side and their child's.
- Be alert and observant, searching for the key to being helpful for each individual child.
- Make a point of writing home or calling with good news.
- Demonstrate your respect for parents as the number-one experts on their own kids. Ask them to share what they know with you for the child's sake.

DR. BRODKIN COMMENTS

This next teacher offers a suggestion about when and how to start enlisting parents' involvement.

BUILDING SUPPORT

At back-to-school night I tell parents, "Look, we're working together here. Your kids are great. We're going to learn. We're going to make this positive, but it doesn't work unless I have your support." Then I draw a triangle, and at each point I say, "You." "Me." "Your child." "This year we've got to work together to keep the learning cycle going. Anybody breaks the support and we don't have as good a chance."

DR. BRODKIN COMMENTS

We can learn a lot from each of these teachers' approaches. Here are valuable tips from other teachers who recommend building trust early on.

STARTING OUT POSITIVE

I make an effort to make at least one positive phone call home to parents very quickly at the beginning of the year, so we have something going before there's a problem. I get a much better reception, because parents have begun to build a trusting relationship with me.

FINDING KEY CLUES

Christopher was a child who was small for his age and very tough. He also adored his stepfather. At one point, his behavior got so bad that I asked the stepfather to come in and stand outside the classroom, just so Christopher would know he was there. Then, after class, his stepfather would come in and talk to me, and this child, this tough child, would go sit in his dad's lap. That really clarified for me who he was and what he was all about. If at all possible, it's just so important that we help children realize that not only do the people at school care what they do here, their parents do, too.

GETTING PARENTS ON YOUR SIDE

I call parents often, especially those who don't come in regularly. If there's a problem, I describe what happened and ask if they can give me any insight, being careful not to lay any blame. After I explain what I'm concerned about, I always say that because they are the ones who have spent so much more time with their child, I'd like to ask them for some assistance. In other words, I'm showing them that I'm convinced that they are working in the best interests of their child at home.

MAKING YOUR POINT

I always read *Leo the Late Bloomer* to parents. It's perfect! And I tell parents, "Your child may learn to read a year later than every other child. But what's the goal? To read. They're going to be reading for the next 80 years, so it's okay if it takes them six months or a year longer. They have a long time to enjoy the skill."

In so many ways, it helps when teachers and parents work together to prevent problems and also to confront them successfully once they have occurred. And as we have seen, there is a direct benefit when children find their parents and teachers collaborating readily on their behalf. But since so many parents bring an old distrust of school to the table, teachers often need to devise clever ways of putting parents at ease. The greatest challenge usually comes when it seems necessary to suggest outside help. Once again, taking a collegial position, and acknowledging the teachers' own need for expert advice, may make even this situation less arduous.

Getting Help

SOME VERY EXPERIENCED AND WISE TEACHERS don't hesitate to call upon experts, such as child-study team members, the school nurse, or trusted teacher colleagues, when a child's problematic behavior puzzles them. And these teachers who face the unique needs of a perplexing child also recognize their own personal need for support. Some find lunchroom brainstorming works for them, while others avoid public discussion and turn instead to an administrator or another staff member. There is no universal "right way," but one way or another, the need for teacher support should be met. The teachers in this chapter share their strategies for finding the support they need in order to best guide children.

LOOK TO OTHER PROFESSIONALS

When there's a problem, the most important thing I do, if at all possible, is involve parents and seek out experts. I rely heavily on my child-study team, whether it's for academic or behavior problems, or concerns I have about the child's welfare at home, even if the problem is that he isn't making friends at school. Yes, I'm the educator, but they are the ones who specialize in social, emotional, and behavioral issues.

RELY ON COLLEAGUES

All the kids at our school are low-income. Everybody gets free field trips, and there are probably only two kids in my room who pay for their lunch. We have a lot of parents in jail, one-parent families, alcoholism and drugs, shootings, stabbings, and killings. And we're all aware that children are getting more violent at a younger age. When I feel frustrated and down, I turn to the other teachers in my building. We talk and vent to each other. We all understand what it's like to teach at our school, and we build on this natural bond.

DR. BRODKIN COMMENTS

Informal support systems are vitally important. Who else but those in the same school can understand the stresses that teachers endure? That goes for teachers in calmer neighborhoods as well. Wherever there are kids and caring, there is joy and there is stress, and teachers need each other to cope better. Read on for more ideas about finding support in your school community.

NETWORK WITH THE PAST

If I'm having behavior or academic problems with a specific student, I usually go to the teachers that student had in the past two years. For instance, if I have someone who's not doing well on tests, I might go to her previous teacher and say, "Did you notice a problem with this last year? What worked for you?" I've also learned that sometimes it's important to find out what the class was like for the child the previous year. I remember a student who wasn't doing well in my room at all. He just couldn't handle the responsibility of making choices. I found out that his previous year had been spent with one of our teachers who is very strict, very old-fashioned in the way she teaches, and this had been good for him. Knowing that and talking to her, I was able to modify some things about his day to help him move into a freer environment more gradually and successfully.

YOU DON'T HAVE TO DO IT ALONE

I've become a firm believer in taking your lunch hour rather than working through it. At our school, it's a time when we can talk, seek ideas, or even vent. And, if a teacher is having a particularly bad day, everyone in the lunchroom is there to listen, to coach, or at least to offer an encouraging word, which I think is invaluable. Then, when you go back into the classroom, problems seem a little bit more tolerable. I've also found that it's vital to have a few people at school I feel connected to so I can talk about issues and concerns with them rather than face the problems alone.

PRINCIPAL SUPPORT

Having a principal who supports you and listens to you is a great help. With my more severe behavior problems, my principal says to me, "If you get to a point where you can't take it, why don't you send him down to me, and give yourself a break." I don't think I have ever taken him up on his offer, but just knowing that I could has relieved some of the pressure.

PARENT SUPPORT

I remember the time I went down to my principal's office and said: "Am I doing a bad job? Why are the parents on my back? I can't do anything more than I'm already doing." And he told me, "You know, for every parent who complains to you, you've got fifteen others who support you." What he said stuck with me, and I repeated it to myself a number of times through the years.

NETWORKING WORKS

I had a child two years ago who didn't respond to any of my strategies. I talked to his parents, I talked to every single resource person I could think of. This child was new to the district, so I couldn't talk to his teacher from last year. I asked the psychologist to come and take a look. I asked the nurse. At one point, I remember asking if he could take a hearing test. I talked to the music teacher and the gym teacher. I asked the art teacher how he was doing in her class. We have a special-ed team, and I asked one of the teachers who I really trust to come in informally. I didn't want to tell her anything beforehand, but I could have talked for hours about how this kid was acting out in my class. He was throwing furniture; he was very aggressive.

Slowly, I began to develop a clearer picture of him. And I learned (the hard way) that when you have a child in your class who is so difficult that you don't know what to do, and *your* techniques aren't working, and his behavior isn't getting any better, you do need to have additional resources. We have formed a committee at our school composed of the reading specialist, an administrator, the nurse, and others. Before I seek out their help, I ask colleagues to observe and give me their feedback. They may either support what I was thinking, tell me I was crazy, or give me an idea of something different to try. I rely on their opinion about whether the problem needs to be looked at by the committee and addressed very seriously with the parents, or if it is a problem of the dynamics of my classroom.

DR. BRODKIN COMMENTS

How nice for this teacher and her students that she feels confident and free enough to seek others' counsel. She recognizes that there are times when we can't be totally objective. She allows for the possibility that the problem may even be a local one—originating in the dynamics of her classroom—leaving no stone unturned in considering the child who was acting out in her class. Sometimes, by merely raising questions with others, we can clarify our own thoughts. Whatever suggestions others make are a bonus. Other teachers share their different approaches to problem-solving in the next two vignettes.

A Private Opinion

When I need to talk or need help, I go to the people who I feel show heart and have good intuition about children. I'm not someone who discusses my difficulties with my kids in the staff lunchroom. Too many people do that, and kids get reputations with other teachers that way. I do my question-asking privately; I think the children deserve this dignity.

Before It's Too Late

Don't wait until February to try to figure out why a child is behaving in a certain way. Don't wait to take action on behavior or learning issues. Now that I have some teaching experience, it's not unusual for me to sign up to talk about two or three of my students with a child-study team by the end of September. Otherwise, a whole year can go by, and you find yourself thinking, "I can't believe I missed that or let that go."

DR. BRODKIN COMMENTS

No matter what your approach to a particular situation, there are some times when nothing works. This is heartbreaking for teachers, but we must all accept that there are some children we just can't reach, no matter how hard we try. Teachers in the next few poignant vignettes share the ways they cope with this discouraging situation.

Letting Go

When I have talked to a child personally, over a long period of time, and gotten nowhere, when it appears he doesn't care, won't talk to me, and just shuts down, I've learned that I must face the fact that I failed, and maybe anyone would have. I had a boy like that a few years ago. We suspected he had an abusive father, and I think he had hardened himself—he simply wouldn't let anybody in. That's when I thought, "Boy, I've pulled out every trick I know. Isn't there any other way I could help him?" Most kids' resistance does break down at some point. They will finally cry or show some emotion. This kid never would. Nothing. I could only think, "This child has built such walls that nobody is ever going to get in." That was a tough one for me, totally unexpected, because over the years, even the toughest kids have come to me and apparently felt safe. I still don't understand why I couldn't get to him. I never will.

He left for a year and then came back to our school. He was happy to see me, but I still couldn't reach him. I wanted to so badly, because I felt that his life was just going to get harder.

SOMETIMES YOU CAN'T DO ANY MORE

I think we did everything we could do for Deshawn. We had meetings with the psychologist and the administrators. They worked with his dad. The psychologist, principal, vice principal, and I met again with the father. I talked to both parents, we did the child-study team, we called Children's Protective Services. I felt like I did everything I could do, short of taking the child out of the home myself, which, of course, wasn't possible. I was so involved and so distraught. I still remember my husband saying to me, "You always said you wouldn't give up until you felt that you had done everything you could." Sadly, by that time, I did finally feel that way.

ACCEPTING REALITY

Sometimes we have to accept the fact that we don't get to accomplish all that we're hoping for with every child. Some of their needs are much greater than we are either professionally or personally equipped to meet, and there is only so much we can do in the actual clock hours of the school day. So we have to remind ourselves that kids aren't only affected by our school environment. No matter how fabulous we can make that, they do go home to another place, and that other place determines so much for them.

WE CAN WIN SOME

In our profession, when we see kids in trouble, we really want to turn them around so that when they walk out of our rooms, they'll be well-balanced, together individuals. I think because there are so many other factors we can't change, we have to know that we can try our best, but we're not always going to reach those kids. Then we have to think about how many kids we *are* successful at reaching.

When to Stop Trying

There are no objective criteria to establish when it's time to say "uncle." In part, this is because of the uniqueness of each child's issues, each teacher's situation, and the interface of these two unpredictable and complex variables. However, through our interviews, it became clear that it is extremely important for each teacher to find some kind of comfortable balance between never letting go at one extreme and becoming prematurely discouraged on the other. Each of us has to be our own best judge, for we are the only ones with all the facts and feelings at hand.

*T*eachers who are both zealous and confident have little difficulty in recognizing when they can use another opinion about a child in trouble. However, it may be a bit more difficult to acknowledge that "you can't win them all." Frankly, it's tough to say you've been licked by other forces in a child's life. But there is a time to let go, however disappointing that might be.

6

The Teacher's Role

MOST OF THE TEACHERS **I** INTERVIEWED defined their roles as reaching far beyond the academic sphere. When they shared their very personal views about such matters, it became apparent that they had in common at least one special quality: the inclination to be reflective. That quality contributed to their success in some uphill teaching situations. It was not only that they didn't give up easily, but that they thought deeply about how to meet the challenges of each individual. The teachers in this chapter share their ideas on their roles and responsibilities as teachers—and their thoughts on how to balance their professional and personal lives.

STRIVING TO UNDERSTAND

I think my role is to go as far as I can. It's not my job only to make sure that children behave and are "quiet" enough so other kids can learn, but to understand why they are being disruptive. I think you have to get to the heart of the matter before you can help the student. And that doesn't always happen. I could try for a year and not get it right. But with the help of parents and child-study teams, and talking it through with the student, I think that my role is to discover where the behavior is coming from or why it's happening, because there's usually a reason.

GOING THE EXTRA MILE

I think you have to go the extra mile, because in the end it pays off for you and the children. Yet, putting my job in perspective is hard for me. I tend to want to spend more hours than I probably should. Sometimes my own children feel I spend more time thinking about the classroom than I do about my family. When I hear that, I know I need to stop and say, "Wait a minute." Still, I struggle with how to make every child feel special. Even though I know I can't really do that for everybody, I try. It's my job to try. It's my way of life. It's who I am, and it's what gives me personal gratification. I'm not doing this work solely for the children. When I see change, it makes me feel good.

AN OBLIGATION

Our role may be limited as far as a child's situation outside the classroom, but rather than say, "He's not learning because of this or that at home," we have an obligation not to walk away from things.

SPEAKING OUT

Elijah had had a very difficult year, so the decision was made to give him another chance to feel successful in kindergarten. This turned out to be a good decision, because the "second time around" he had a great school experience. That first year, he had been perceived, by the secretary, the gym teacher, the science teacher, the music teacher, the art teacher, the lunchroom aides, in short, everyone, as a very problematic kid. I felt it was my role to go around to each of the other teachers who had worked with him, as his behavior had improved, and be very up front. "Gee", I'd say, "hasn't Eli been great lately?" I wanted them to say it out loud to me. I wanted to redefine him outside of my classroom to the other people who were working with him. And that happened.

DO WHAT YOU CAN—THEN LET IT GO

Latisha, my student who was gifted, began to take much delight in helping me teach, and eventually took an active role in the class, but she was pulled out of school the following year. Her parents decided to teach her at home. I wrote to her, and she wrote me back saying that she was very unhappy because she didn't think she was learning and hated her situation with a vengeance. I felt it was my responsibility to call her parents and tell them that I didn't think it was working, and Latisha needed to be in school. They said, "No, you're wrong. Look how smart she is now."

I think I did the best I could for Latisha, and I think she really enjoyed her year with me, in our class, at school. It was very hard to see her go, because I knew she wouldn't be back.

DOING THE BEST YOU CAN

I feel I often play the role of mother, teacher, nurse, doctor, every meaningful adult in a child's life. There are so many things we do. You get to the point where you say, "I can't save them all, but I still do the best I can."

TRYING AGAIN AND AGAIN

It's just trial and error—that's what you do with kids all the time, trial and error. And you learn from your mistakes, and you move on.

DRAWING THE LINE

I have had years when I would occasionally just shut the door and cry. Those were years when I had so many kids with problems, and I was doing my best, but doing my best still wasn't good enough. That's really hard. It's hard because teaching is one of those jobs that you could work 24 hours a day and still feel as though you're not putting in the necessary time. Years ago, the school secretary, with whom I had become friends, told me, "Your own kids are only going to be young once. You really need to think about them." And that hit me hard. I decided then not to go to school on weekends, but to do my extra work at home at night. Still, if you go by our school on Sunday, you'll see ten cars in the parking lot, and they will be teachers' cars.

Tips for Guiding Children

Often, opportunities to turn problematic behavior around can be found in simple everyday situations. Some of the teachers who were perceptive enough to discover these at-hand devices, and courageous enough to try them, generously shared their experiences with us. You might want to try any or all of the strategies described just ahead. Some will work with one child, some with another. One day they all may work; another day they may not be as successful. We are, after all, talking about changing the behavior of members of the most complex species on Earth.

COUNT TO FIVE

I had one student who would get in terrible altercations with other students and become verbally abusive. We worked together to help him realize when those feelings were building, and figured out strategies he could use to gain self-control. This is what ended up working:

1. Count to ten;
2. Take a deep breath and walk away for a while;
3. Take a few minutes to pull yourself together;
4. Ask yourself: Do I still feel the same way, and is that where I really want to go with this?
5. Come back to the group.

THREE IMPORTANT QUESTIONS

I keep three questions on the board:

1. Is it safe?
2. Does it promote learning?
3. Is it kind?

If children can look at what they're doing or want to do and answer *yes* to each one, then that's fine. If they answer *no* to even one, then they've gone beyond the line.

WORK WITH CHILDREN

When you want a child to go talk to a counselor, and that child doesn't want to go, try negotiating: "I'd like you to go, and if you don't like it after three times, come and tell me, and I will take you out." You just have to make sure you support the child 100 percent.

POST POSITIVE MESSAGES

To help build a community in our classroom, we spend time talking about "put-downs" and "put-ups." I ask kids to help me make a list of phrases that make people feel good or encourage them to continue what they're doing. I write these on sentence strips, and then we put the strips all over the room so everyone can refer to them. It works! For instance, I've seen a child look at the strips, think a minute, and turn to another child and simply say, "Good job." Coming from a teacher that might sound pretty shallow, but from a child to a child, it's pretty powerful.

MAILBOX INSIGHTS

I keep a little mailbox in my room and explain to children that when they have something they want to say to me that they might not feel comfortable saying out loud, they can write it in a note and put it in the mailbox. For instance, I had one child write, "I can't sit next to so-and-so any more." Then I made the appropriate change.

NEGOTIATE

I had one child with exceptional problems who would burst into tears when I told the class what I wanted them to do. His situation was very complex, and I had to learn to deal with him in a way that made sense for the whole class. Over a period of a few months I taught him the word "negotiate," and worked out this arrangement: When I gave the whole class an assignment, I winked at him to remind him that he and I would negotiate. After the other kids started working, he could come to my desk and say, "Okay, let's negotiate."

Here is why I think this worked: I truly believe that most kids want to do exactly what you ask them to do. And, all kids want to succeed. When a child is at the point where he or she needs to negotiate, it's for a good reason—that child simply can't do what you're asking. So the adult has to make it turn out to be successful. Negotiating helps with that, and most kids take to negotiating like the proverbial duck to water.

DR. BRODKIN COMMENTS

This is the embodiment of those vital ingredients which seem to promote progress: empathy, listening to and respecting the child's view, banishing the child's sense of powerlessness, supporting the teacher-child relationship, and enabling the child to know that this important adult believes in him and that he and his ideas do matter.

TAKE TIME TO REGROUP

When I'm at my wits' end, I have an arrangement that allows the child who's driving me up the wall to go to another classroom (to sit) for 15 minutes. That gives me a chance to regroup, and it does the same for the child. Also, when I see a child starting to lose control, I say, "Would you please deliver this?" The delivery is an envelope with nothing inside, but it gives the child a chance to leave the room. And sometimes just leaving the class, walking to another room and coming back, can pull a child together.

POINTING OUT THE POSITIVE

I have a "Gift of Time" plan which I write on the board. It starts with recognizing what kids are doing correctly. I explain: "You've earned five seconds for the class because you've continued to work through this interruption," or, "You've earned twenty seconds for the class because you waited until so-and-so finished talking before you asked a question," or, "You've all earned five minutes because you've been so patient with me this morning." This plan really comes through for me when I feel like I'm getting crabby or annoyed. It helps me do an about-face and point out the positives in children's behavior. Everyone wants to be the one I'm speaking of, although I never identify anyone by name.

ORCHESTRATING SEATING ARRANGEMENTS

I had a group of students in one class, all of whom had the potential to be disruptive. In fact, as a group they often became extremely disruptive. I like to teach on the rug, but when they got there, I couldn't get anything done. They were always hitting, laughing, pointing, and pulling. So I put each person's name on an "X" on the rug, deliberately separating particular disruptive duos and trios. I also learned to put kids close to me so that I could reach out and touch most of them if I had to support their shaky self-control.

BUDDY UP!

We have a great buddy program at our school. Adults in the building pair up with kids who are having problems and try to get together at least once a month. (I think some people do it even more than that.) Individual pairs have lunch together and just try to keep on top of things. A classroom teacher isn't ever a buddy to a kid in his or her own class. We also try to make sure that each buddy is someone the kid would identify with and be able to talk to about things other than school.

DR. BRODKIN COMMENTS

Buddy programs like the one in the last story provide another opportunity for each child to feel valued, listened to, and believed in, and they provide an opportunity to have a benevolent role model, someone with whom it is easy and fun to relate and share interests. This is the stuff from which genuine self-esteem can grow.

PRIVATE TIME

If someone's really out of line during a time when everyone is supposed to be working in an organized way, like when I'm doing reading groups, I'll ask that person to put his or her name on the board. This serves as a warning. If I have to say the person's name again, that child has to come up and put a check next to it. That little check means he owes me two minutes of lunchtime recess. It's not so much the time that's the big thing, but the fact that the person has to come in the classroom during lunch when I'm there alone and we have a chance to talk, and I have an opportunity to do a little individualized counseling.

This has been an interesting process. Sometimes I'll have kids go up to the board when they don't think I'm watching, and write their names with check marks just so they can come in and talk. It seems there is no disgrace about being expected to come for my guidance. In fact, it may be looked upon as a privilege to get some private time with me.

PAIR OLDER KIDS WITH YOUNGER ONES

I had five or six kids in my class who were pretty much nonreaders. I chose a kindergarten class to work with because I figured my kids who were having difficulty with reading at their level could read simple books to those children. It worked! My fourth graders felt important because they were helping the younger kids read. Even my toughest kids felt smart, successful, and looked up to because they were important and smart to somebody else. And I could praise them for what they were achieving.

DR. BRODKIN COMMENTS

Many of these teachers' successful strategies rely on the power of praise, which we have underscored a number of times. But what is more, these tactics build confidence through genuine opportunities for success. Nothing succeeds in turning a child around like the personal experience of success, followed by well-earned praise.

RECIPE FOR SUCCESS

It may sound simple, but here's a cardinal rule: Find something children can be successful at, and let them be successful at it. Maybe there's a job a child could do every day, even just a little job. In other words, set kids up for success, and then you get to tell them, "Hey, look at what you did. That was great!"

CARING COUNTS

Last year I had one of the most problematic kids I've ever had—a girl whose name was Dominique. Dominique's mother was in jail, and she lived with her aunt, who may not have been the best influence, because she had a pretty shady existence herself. Dominique tended to be vulgar in front of the class, throw things, and occasionally she would come up and put her elbows on my desk, lean in three inches from my face, and just stare and stare at me. She wouldn't even move when I asked her to.

I made a decision to spend time with her after school. (I know this is not a great solution because we can't do this with all our students, but I didn't know what else to do.) I told her that if she got her act together and acted like a lady for three weeks, we would go out for dinner. She did it! We went out for dinner, and a few weeks later we went to a movie. I ended up taking her three or four places. We even went to the *Nutcracker* at Christmastime.

Her teacher this year is having problems with her again, but Dominique's behavior is still better than it was last year. I still talk to her, and she responds to me, I think, because I showed her that I really care about her, and I helped her learn how to behave. I just told it to her like it was, and by spending time together outside of school, she began to understand more about how people act and relate to each other.

DR. BRODKIN COMMENTS

While it is rarely practical to rely on out-of-school time spent with a child, some of the same principles can be applied within the school day. Consider examples we have already heard, about private chats at lunchtime or after school, the other-teacher buddy system, and even in-class negotiating or individualized interaction. All of these provide the benefits of special quality time and include various nonacademic learning, modeling, and social mentoring opportunities.

MAKE A PLAN TOGETHER

The first moment I notice a problem in a child's behavior, I get busy looking for the really great things about that kid, showcasing what he or she is good at, and minimizing the situations and the kinds of things that bring negative attention to the behavior. Because that's not always possible, I also try to give the child alternative behavior strategies. We talk about what the specific problematic behavior is and make a plan together. A plan for one child might be: "How am I going to get better at raising my hand and not interrupting?" or, "How am I going to get better at thinking about what I want to say before I say it?" or, "How can I let other people have a turn, or use words so that I get what I want, but in a positive way so other kids will want to play with me?"

MAKING ALLIES

I had one child who always got in trouble when I wasn't watching—poking other kids, clowning around. So when we walked down the hall (a time when this behavior often took place), I had him hold my hand at the front of the line. I didn't want this to be a punishment, so I said, "You know, I have a funny feeling that if you hold my hand when we walk down the hall, this class is going to behave beautifully. Let's see if it works." And it did work for him! The first few times I fussed over him, and there was a distinct difference in the class—they behaved. So then I said to him while we were walking, "This is like magic. All I have to do is hold your hand and everyone behaves." He never balked; instead, he would run to get to the front and hold my hand!

DR. BRODKIN COMMENTS

This child sounds like others I have known who have concluded that "getting in trouble" is the only way to get attention. That notion may have arisen elsewhere, but was then reinforced by some school experiences. The teacher, in this instance, avoided the opportunity for more of the same, and, at the same time, communicated a sense of the child's value and importance to her.

USING CHARACTERS IN BOOKS

I always try to think about the characters' behaviors when we read stories, and I ask children what they think: "Why do you think so many people in the class like Arthur?" "Why do you think so many in the class didn't like Francine?" "What kinds of things did Francine do that made people not like her?" This kind of discussion, based on children's literature, is really important and meaningful.

When I have a kid who never hears directions and is always in the wrong place at the wrong time, I'll give him directions and then ask pointedly, "Now what are you supposed to do?" Having a child repeat to you what is expected can make him tune in a little bit better and get him in the habit of seeing a need to listen to the instructions.

DR. BRODKIN COMMENTS

This could be a child who has auditory processing problems and/or sequencing problems, which often turn out to explain such apparent inattentiveness and difficulty with multi-step directions. It is important to identify any such underlying problem in order to remediate it, and to avoid damage to the child's self-esteem.

Dr. Stanley Greenspan and his colleagues have devised a "dimensional approach" to understanding and working with children who have specific challenges. It is an approach that builds understanding of the child's functioning and designs interventions based on that understanding. He recommends looking at:

- The child's ability to communicate and relate.

- The way the child processes sensations, including sights, sounds, and touch.

- The way the child plans and carries out actions (including following directions).

- The developmental stage of the child, including emotional, social, and intellectual development.

- The child's interaction with family members.

Once these things are assessed with the help of an expert, the teacher and parent can carry out an intervention plan to improve whatever needs improvement. The observant teacher is the one who can best fill out the child's profile of functioning.

Two more teachers offer valuable hints in the following vignettes.

WHERE IS YOUR ATTENTION GOING?

At the end of each day, especially in September, I jot down (on my roll-call list) the personal contact I've had with each child—something I said personally to them. Then I take time to ask myself: Are there any children I didn't have some personal one-to-one dialogue with? The process has given me a better idea of who the withdrawn children are, who the children are who seek the most attention, and where *my* energy and attention are going.

MAKING SENSE OF RULES

I am careful not to keep changing the rules on kids or to make new rules in reaction to children's behavior. Kids need to understand what the expectations and boundaries are, and why. I find it works best to relate children's behavior to the rules I have clearly established with them. Being consistent and predictable avoids confusion.

DR. BRODKIN COMMENTS

This is a very helpful observation. Somehow we need to strive for consistency without rigidity. Children, as we have said before, thrive on clear expectations and boundaries of acceptable behavior. Their thinking, especially in the primary years, is still quite concrete, and they feel safest when they can predict your reactions to their behavior. At the same time, however, teachers can use their own good judgment about how they can be firm, but kind. In certain ambivalent situations, it pays to listen to explanations from those involved before deciding the rules have been broken.

CONTROLLED FREEDOM

I don't like it when I'm working with one group of students and we keep getting interrupted by other kids saying things like: "Can I sharpen my pencil?" "Can I go to the bathroom?" So I've worked out these procedures. If students want to sharpen their pencils, they put their pencil tip in the air. Then all I have to do is look and nod, and they can get up and go. There's no verbal communication. I don't get interrupted with my reading group, and they don't get off task and bother the kid next to them. It's a little thing, but it works like a charm, and it sets the tone of respecting working time. With the bathroom, I use a pass. There's only one. The kids can use it whenever they want, with the exception of when I'm actually instructing, like during a math lesson. Otherwise they have that "controlled freedom."

DR. BRODKIN COMMENTS

"Controlled Freedom" is a wonderful phrase and a useful concept for teachers and for parents. I suspect there would be much less rebellious behavior if children could feel they have a voice about their own interests, within the limits of adult-devised parameters. A child's wish for autonomy is healthy and bodes well for future achievement. We shouldn't fear it, but instead guide it within safe waters whenever possible.

A WORD FROM THE WISE

Give kids choices, but be sure to limit them to choices you can live with.

USE AN INTERPRETER!

Sometimes I'll be teaching and get frustrated because I know the kids aren't getting it, and they're getting restless, so I ask a kid who does understand to come up and explain it in "kid language."

DR. BRODKIN COMMENTS

More wonderful advice. Teachers must often be inventive and open-minded to succeed. The guideline we gain here is: "When necessary, aim for getting your message across on the kids' own terms."

FOSTER RECOGNITION

I'm always encouraging kids to be positive about one another. I have this thing called IALAC, which stands for "I am loving and caring." When kids see somebody doing something nice, they go up to the board and write it down. For instance, "I saw Jake opening the door for Ms. Herman." In other words, they have to find nice things about one another, and they know that by the end of the month, I hope to see everybody's name up there. I might say, "I don't see any Darrens up there; let's watch Darren for a while." Or I might say, "Somebody watch Darren, somebody watch Carolina, and somebody watch Antonio, and see if you can catch them doing something nice." The whole process is a real shot in the arm for everyone.

OFFER KIDS A FRESH PERSPECTIVE

Once a month I change the way the desks in my room are arranged. Not just where kids sit, but how the desks are positioned. Sometimes it's for behavior reasons, sometimes it's a science unit where I need small groups, or sometimes I just want lots of space in the middle of the room. The custodian can't stand it. He says he never knows which way to push his broom. But it's one more way to keep kids on their toes and thinking all the time, and it sometimes just brings us a fresh perspective.

PRIVACY MATTERS

At my school, kids can fill out blue slips if they'd like to speak with a counselor. Sometimes, to encourage a child I'll say, "This might be something you'd like to talk to Mrs. so-and-so about. Why don't you fill out a blue slip?" I always remind them privately that anything they say is personal and confidential between them and the counselor.

JOURNALING

From the beginning of the year, I let children know that anything they put in their journals is just between the two of us, unless it's something that's about hurting themselves or someone else. For instance, I explain, "If you tell me that you're going to have to beat up someone after school, then I have a problem, and I have to take care of that because somebody's going to get hurt." This process builds trust, and I have been able to learn so much about my students in this way. One girl really opened up to me, and we wrote back and forth to each other. There were certain things I showed the guidance counselor; the girl didn't know about this reporting because it fell under the category of helping her not hurt herself.

> **DR. BRODKIN COMMENTS**
>
> Some children, who would not feel free to talk about worries, will enact them in play or write about them, particularly if they sense the observer or reader might provide help. It's a valid way of reaching out—and a step forward toward greater trust of the teacher.

COUNTERING NEGATIVE BEHAVIOR

When a kid has a behavior problem, like being a bully, chances are he's been getting negative input about himself at home and from his peers, too. It takes a lot of work from me to help the child recognize when he's doing things successfully so he has a chance to repeat that positive behavior. I've found that it helps to put a little chart on the child's desk so I can come by and note things he is doing well. This certainly helps build his awareness—and mine—that he does do good things.

DR. BRODKIN COMMENTS

Here, once again, we have inspiring evidence of inventiveness and a relentless quest to help the kids grow. In the process, teachers help themselves to grow.

LET CHILDREN PICK THEIR MENTORS

If a child is having difficulties, I ask if there is another child (or more than one) in the room who he feels makes choices that work well—someone who gets his or her work done or has fun at recess, but doesn't seem to have a lot of "time outs." Then we talk about what that child does. Sometimes the child will request that one of those children be, essentially, a peer mentor or playmate. If so, I speak to the potential mentor privately, saying, "Here's what so-and-so noticed about you. I'm wondering if you would consider letting him sit with you sometimes to do some learning and watching, and to get to feel good that he's with someone who makes good choices." However, I always give the potential child mentor the choice of whether or not to participate.

THE BENEFITS OF REFLECTING

Throughout the year I try to keep this personal rule with children and adults: I tell myself to work very hard to be in control of myself, watch my body language, and be aware of any other nonverbal cues that might give a message I don't want to convey. I also really try to take time to think about who I am and whether my philosophy and classroom goals are clear. I've found this helps me avoid inappropriate, spontaneous responses to situations. I'm very even-tempered, but I didn't just get this way. It was a deliberate choice I made, and I have worked hard at it.

DR. BRODKIN COMMENTS

Even the most experienced and gifted teacher (or for that matter, anyone who works at enabling others to grow) does best if he or she engages in ongoing reflective thinking. We need to understand ourselves if we are to enable others to do the same. Such mental processing of behavior before the fact is what we are all hoping to encourage in children. When we expect the same of ourselves, we gain greater respect for the challenge.

COLLABORATION WORKS!

Our entire school feels that teamwork is important. After the new class lists come out, we go to former teachers, and they communicate what has worked with specific kids and what hasn't. We can also come back to each other and say, "I tried this and this and it hasn't worked; can you think of something you did that was really successful?" We've found that collaboration like this on behalf of our kids is crucial. Otherwise, working with a child can be like several people doing a jigsaw puzzle by themselves, each with missing pieces—the child gets one thing from one teacher and something else from another without any carryover. Without this kind of continuity, it's even more difficult for kids who have problems, and they can end up going through school with less help and more negative labels.

DR. BRODKIN COMMENTS

There has been so much said about not reading children's records in order to avoid preconceived notions. And, to some extent, that's useful advice. But this teacher adds another important dimension: knowing how to go about being informed about data that has been gathered already. There is great merit in hearing what others who have been involved have thought, done, or are doing, by sharing what has or has not been effective, then freeing your mind to observe and evaluate the situation, plan a course of action, and eventually, work as a team of school personnel, experts, and family on the child's behalf. In other words, be informed, keep an open mind, and trust your insight. But always, for optimum results, we try to combine private reflection with teamwork in the best interest of children's behavioral development.

Throughout this book I have referred to two remarkable characteristics of the teachers I interviewed. The first is their inclination to step back and reflect about each child's particular situation. The second is a related determination to design an approach unique to each child's needs. As you think about these teachers' experiences and observations, and compare them with your own, you might be guided by some key questions they asked themselves:

- Why is this child acting this way?

- Is the child aware that his or her behavior is problematic?

- Does the child behave in the same way when that child is elsewhere in the school environment?

- Is the behavior occurring every day at the same time, under the same circumstances?

- Could there be things going on at school, even perhaps within my own classroom, that I am not aware of?

- What might be going on in his life outside of school?

- Might it help to talk with the child's parents/family members, especially to learn whether they see the child's behavior as problematic at home, too?

- Is there anyone in the school community whom I should ask to observe this child?

- Who else might help me to think this through?

- Why does the behavior bother me so?

- Do others also see it as problematic?

- Knowing what I do about the child and his or her life, how can I intervene and guide that child toward greater comfort in the classroom and more appropriate behavior?

These questions seem to have served the teachers whom we interviewed well, and they may be a good place for you to begin your own inquiry about any child's problematic behavior. But please, don't stop there. In the end, trust your own instincts and the advice of your trusted colleagues. The work you do is vital to developing human beings, and it will be best served by drawing on your own special vision.

Anthony, E. James, and Bertram J. Cohler, eds. *The Invulnerable Child.* The Guilford Press, 1987.

Beane, Allan L. *The Bully Free Classroom, Over 100 Tips and Strategies for Teachers K–8.* Free Spirit Publishing, 1999.

Boyer, Ernest L. *The Basic School, A Community for Learning.* The Carnegie Foundation for the Advancement of Teaching, 1995.

Brodkin, Adele M. "When It's Time to Get Help." *Instructor Magazine,* Nov/Dec, 1991: 10–11.

Collins, W. Andrew, ed. *Development During Middle Childhood: The Years from Six to Twelve.* National Academy Press, 1984.

Comer, James P. *Child by Child: The Comer Process for Change in Education.* Teachers College Press, 1999.

————. *Waiting for a Miracle: Why Schools Can't Solve Our Problems—And How We Can.* Dutton, 1997.

————. *Rallying the Whole Village: The Comer Process for Reforming Education.* Teachers College Press, 1996.

————. *Maggie's American Dream.* New American Library, 1988.

————. "Public Education: We Must Make It Work," The Search for Effective Schools, A Conference in Honor of Roy E. Larsen, *Harvard Graduate School of Education Association Bulletin,* vol. XXV, no. 1, Fall 1980: 36–37.

————. "Schools as a Family Support System," *International Year of the Child,* Child Advocacy 1979: Proceedings, Yale University, June 21–22, 1979, Susan Lustman Katz (ed.), Child Study Center, Yale University.

————. "Parent Participation and Urban Schools," *School Social Work Quarterly,* vol. 1, no. 4, Winter 1979–80: 309–325.

Cummings, E. Mark, and Patrick Davies. *Children and Marital Conflict.* The Guilford Press, 1994.

Edwards, C. Drew. *How to Handle a Hard-To-Handle Kid: A Parents' Guide to Understanding and Changing Problem Behaviors.* Free Spirit Publishing, 1988.

Emery, Robert E. *Marriage, Divorce, and Children's Adjustment,* 2nd edition. Sage Publications, 1999.

Eisenberg, Nancy, and Janet Strayer, eds. *Empathy and Its Development.* Cambridge University Press, 1987.

Garbarino, James, et. al. *Children in Danger.* Jossey-Bass, 1992.

Goldstein, Joseph, Albert J. Solnit, et al. *The Best Interests of the Child.* Free Press, 1996.

Goleman, Daniel. *Emotional Intelligence.* Bantam, 1995.

Greenspan, Stanley I. *The Challenging Child.* Addison Wesley, 1995.

————. *Playground Politics.* Addison Wesley, 1993.

Kazdin, Alan E. *Conduct Disorders in Childhood and Adolescence*, 2nd edition. Sage Publications,1995.

Kirkland, Lynn. "The Role of Autonomy in the Elementary Classroom," *ACEI Focus on Elementary*, Fall 1999, Vol. 12, #1.

Letts, Nancy. *Creating a Caring Classroom.* Scholastic Professional Books, 1997.

Little, Mary. "Creating Caring Classroom Communities: At the Heart of Education," *ACEI Focus on Elementary*, Winter 1998, Vol. 11, #2.

McLanahan, Sara, and Gary Sandefur. *Growing Up with a Single Parent, What Hurts, What Helps.* Harvard University Press, 1994.

Miller, Frank. "Helping the Overly Aggressive Child Develop Pro-Social Behavior," *ACEI Focus on Pre-K & K*, Summer 1998, Vol. 10, #4.

Newman, Fran. *Children in Crisis: Support for Teachers and Parents.* Scholastic, 1993.

Novick, Rebecca. "Fostering Resiliency and Emotional Intelligence," *Childhood Education*, Summer 1998: 200–204.

Olweus, Dan. *Bullying at School.* Blackwell, 1995.

Porter, Louise. *Young Children's Behavior.* Maclennan and Petty, 2000.

Ramsey, Patricia G. *Making Friends in School.* Teachers College Columbia University Press, 1991.

Riley, Sue Spayth. *How to Generate Values in Young Children.* National Association for the Education of Young Children, 1984.

Rogers, Bill. *Cracking the Hard Class.* Scholastic, 1997.

————. *Behavior Management.* Ashton Scholastic, 1995.

Stone, Jeannette Galambos. *A Guide to Discipline*, revised edition. NAEYC, 1997.

Terr, Lenore. *Too Scared to Cry.* Harper & Row, 1990.

Visher, Emily B., and John S. Visher. *Stepfamilies: A Guide to Working with Stepparents and Stepchildren.* Brunner/Mazel, 1979.

Wenning, Kenneth. *Winning Cooperation from Your Child: A Comprehensive Method to Stop Defiant and Aggressive Behavior in Children.* Jason Aronson, 1996.

Windle, Michael, and John S. Searles, eds. *Children of Alcoholics.* The Guilford Press, 1990.

Winnicott, D. W. *Deprivation and Delinquency.* Tavistock Publications, 1984.